FUZZY SETS, NATURAL LANGUAGE COMPUTATIONS, AND RISK ANALYSIS

OTHER BOOKS OF INTEREST
FROM COMPUTER SCIENCE PRESS

Jean-Loup Baer
Computer Systems Architecture

Peter Calingaert
Assemblers, Compilers, and Program Translation

M. Carberry, H. Khalil, J. Leathrum, and L. Levy
Foundations of Computer Science

Shimon Even
Graph Algorithms

Ellis Horowitz and Sartaj Sahni
Fundamentals of Computer Algorithms

Ellis Horowitz
Fundamentals of Programming Languages, Second Edition

Ellis Horowitz and Sartaj Sahni
Fundamentals of Data Structures

Ellis Horowitz and Sartaj Sahni
Fundamentals of Data Structures in Pascal

Thomas Logsdon
Computers and Social Controversy

Theo Pavlidis
Algorithms for Graphics and Image Processing

Ira Pohl and Alan Shaw
The Nature of Computation: An Introduction to Computer Science

Arto Salomaa
Jewels of Formal Language Theory

Donald D. Spencer
Computers in Number Theory

FUZZY SETS, NATURAL LANGUAGE COMPUTATIONS, AND RISK ANALYSIS

KURT J. SCHMUCKER
The George Washington University

Foreword by Lotfi A. Zadeh

COMPUTER SCIENCE PRESS

Computer Science Press
11 Taft Court
Rockville, Maryland 20850

1 2 3 4 5 6 Printing   Year 89 88 87 86 85 84

Library of Congress Cataloging in Publication Data

Schmucker, Kurt J.
  Fuzzy sets, natural language computations, and risk analysis.

  Bibliography:
  Includes indexes.
  1. Fuzzy sets. 2. Risk. 3. Language and languages.
I. Title.
QA248.S345 1984   511.3'22   82-23648
ISBN 0-914894-83-8

To Karen

'Defendit numerus' [there is safety in numbers]
is the maxim of the foolish;

'Deperdit numerus' [there is ruin in numbers]
of the wise.

C.C. Colton (1820)

CONTENTS

LIST OF ILLUSTRATIONS

FOREWORD

The traditional approaches to risk analysis are based on the premise that probability theory provides the necessary and sufficient tools for dealing with the uncertainty and imprecision which underlie the concept of risk in decision analysis.

The theory of fuzzy sets calls into question the validity of this premise. More specifically, it suggests that much of the uncertainty which is intrinsic in risk analysis is rooted in the fuzziness of the information which is resident in the database and, more particularly, in the fuzziness of the underlying probabilities. Viewed in this perspective, then, it is the failure of classical probability theory to come to grips with the issue of fuzziness of data that limits its effectiveness in dealing with a wide variety of problem areas—including risk analysis—in which some of the principal sources of uncertainty are nonstatistical in nature.

In applying the theory of fuzzy sets to the analysis of real-world problems, it is natural to adopt the view that imprecision in primary data should, in general, induce commensurate imprecision in the results of the analysis. It is, basically, this view that motivated the introduction of the concept of a linguistic variable, that is, a variable whose values are not numbers but words or sentences in a natural or synthetic language. The theory of fuzzy sets provides a framework for dealing with such variables in a systematic way and thereby opens the door to the application of the linguistic approach in a wide variety of problem areas which do not lend themselves to precise analysis in the classical spirit.

Professor Lance Hoffman and his associate Don Clements were the first to explore the application of the theory of fuzzy sets—and, more particularly, the linguistic approach—to privacy, security and risk analysis. The present monograph is an outgrowth of this effort. It serves to introduce the reader to the theory of fuzzy sets and explains clearly and with many examples the use of the linguistic approach. Mr. Schmucker deserves to be complimented for presenting a coherent and self-contained account of a body of concepts and techniques which are of considerable relevance to risk analysis and natural language computations, and for contributing many insights which facilitate their application to the solution of practical problems.

L. A. Zadeh
Berkeley
April 1982

AUTHOR'S PREFACE

The intellectual task of analyzing the risk present in any large undertaking is an endeavor that abounds both with inherent imprecision and with a scarcity of historical data. Traditional mathematical and computational methods offer little to aid the analyst in work beset with either of these two difficulties, let alone work that is plagued by both of them. This is because the basic philosophical system upon which our mathematics and computer science is based is discrete and adheres strictly to the principle of the excluded middle: a statement must either be true or false. Unfortunately, this is rarely the case in risk analysis.

Fortunately, there is an alternative to this philosophy. This alternative, fuzzy set theory, is aimed at the development of tools for the solution of problems too complex or too ill-defined to be susceptible to analysis by conventional methods. This text provides the reader with an introduction to fuzzy set theory and explains one example of the use of that theory in risk analysis: the use of natural language expressions for the estimation of risk. An existing experimental automated risk analyzer which embodies these techniques is also described in some detail and future research directions are outlined.

This text will be useful to both students and professionals in a variety of disciplines and occupations: to the computer scientist it presents a readable introduction to a current topic in computer security and risk analysis and presents an application of the principles of abstract data structures considerably more involved than the stacks and queues usually presented in introductory courses; to the mathematician it presents an application of the results of an esoteric branch of mathematics, fuzzy set theory, to a practical problem that is becoming increasingly more important today; to the linguist it presents an application of the "linguistic approach" to a problem traditionally the forte of numerical scientists, as well as presenting a technique for the modeling of natural language expressions—a modeling which is both theoretically sound and experimentally verified. The common theoretical underpinning of these diverse fields is mathematics, and it is assumed that all readers will possess the mathematical maturity that is gained, for instance, from an undergraduate education in engineering or the physical sciences.

It is hoped that this text will be an introduction to the idea of automatic risk analysis utilities for those who require only an overview of this current research area, as well as a gentle introduction to the supporting literature for those who would extend the research frontiers. Both groups need to see "the big picture." Hopefully, this little text presents such a view.

K.J.S.
Washington, D.C.
November 1982

ACKNOWLEDGMENTS

The author wishes to acknowledge the contribution of both the scholarship and the camaraderie of the George Washington University Computer Security Research Group to the production of this text. That group provided an exceptionally fertile ground for the discussion of future plans, the correction of old errors, and the presentation of these ideas to the uninitiated end user. Special mention must also be made of the assistance of the group's leader, Lance Hoffman, and the group's other mathematician, Jerry Gaskill. Both suffered through the many drafts and supplied the author with numerous corrections and words of encouragement. The students of CSCI 229 ("Security & Privacy in Computer Systems") at The George Washington University used the manuscript version of this text in their course and provided me with many corrections and suggestions. Rich Atkinson spent a Christmas vacation poring over the final draft and suggested many rewordings and additions. Terry Ireland checked the syntax of the Pascal procedures and advised me on the best format style. My thanks to all for their assistance.

INTRODUCTION

The rigorous determination of the amount of risk associated with a particular proposed endeavor is a topic of both great practical and theoretical interest. It is of theoretical interest because it is an unsolved and difficult problem. It is of practical interest because the risks associated with many important projects are potentially serious and have ramifications throughout our society. Two examples where the determination of risk is both difficult and important are: (1) the risk to human life in a space launch and (2) the risk of compromise of personal data stored in a computer system. To be able somehow to reasonably estimate the risk to human life associated with as complex and multi-faceted an undertaking as a space launch would aid technicians and managers alike in evaluating tradeoffs for safety that must be made both before and during the launch. Similarly, to be able to meaningfully estimate the risk of compromise to confidential personal data in a computer system is essential in deciding on the security measures to be installed on the system and the security practices to be followed by its users.

At first glance, the determinations needed in these two examples appear extremely difficult, if not impossible. This difficulty lies in two completely separate phenomena: overall complexity and inherent imprecision. In the space launch problem, for example, suppose that you have been asked to estimate the risk associated with the launch *in toto* and that afterwards you have to decide how much safety equipment to purchase. The overall environment of a space launch is a complex arrangement of dependent interlocking events. The cognitive overload on a person who must estimate some important quantity based on data for the entire system is staggering. More often than not, a human is forced to neglect many facets of the total problem in order to delimit a manageable set of the data. Unfortunately, this can result in the ignoring of data ultimately important to the overall result, thereby providing a suboptimal (or even a totally wrong!) estimate. Such a suboptimal estimate can result in a considerable danger being overlooked or, alternatively, can force the use of unnecessary and costly safety equipment and procedures.

Even if the complexity problem was solved, the other problem of inherent imprecision remains to complicate the task of estimating risk. Suppose in the computer security example mentioned above that you have been asked to estimate the probability of one specific type of security failure: the unauthorized access of an intruder to the main computer room—a room whose only entrance is equipped with a cypher lock. (For those unacquainted with such a device, a cypher lock is a mechanical device consisting of an array of ten buttons or toggle switches which, when a certain sequence of five buttons is pressed, opens a door. Such a device is used to limit access to a restricted area that has a heavy flow of traffic in and out. It is functionally similar to the more common key lock with the advantage that it is much easier to change the combination of a cypher lock than it is to change the key for a key lock.) If one forgets for a moment the case where one of the authorized individuals knowingly lets an intruder into the facility, the only case you have to consider is that in which somehow the intruder was able to get by the electro-mechanical device controlling access, the cypher lock. Since the cypher lock has 10 buttons, and since any combination that activates the cypher lock (thereby opening the door) is a certain sequence of five buttons, you could estimate that there are 100,000 possible combinations and that, therefore, the probability that an outsider might guess the right combination in one try is 1/100,000, in two tries 2/100,000, etc. Since your particular cypher lock allows only two incorrect tries before covering the presumed imposter in seven gallons of indelible yellow foam and sounding an alarm that would wake the dead, you feel pretty secure. Unfortunately, this estimate (and this entire methodology for estimating) neglects the time when someone spilled a Coke into the cypher lock and *any* combination opened the door, as well as the time when a disgruntled computer operator, having been covered in yellow foam the week before, painted the correct combination on the wall just above the lock *and* it took your ever vigilant security office more than two weeks to notice it!

The problem with your precise estimate of the probability of an intruder gaining access is that it possesses only a pseudo-accuracy—it looks great to the casual observer, but it fails to take into account perturbations that are *possible* in the real world—perturbations that are in some sense likely, taking into account Murphy's Second Law! ("If things can possibly go wrong, they will; if they can't possibly go wrong they still will—and in spades!" (This is also known as the Titanic effect.)) These real-world events are ignored in the "precise" analysis because it is unrealistic to calculate the *probability* of an intruder gaining access—there just isn't sufficient data for such a mathematically precise estimate. All one can reasonably estimate is the *possibility* or the *plausibility* of such an event taking place, given the information that you can have on hand or can reasonably assemble. Realizing this inherent lack of precise and complete data, it would seem (at least at first glance) that rather than estimating the probability of an intruder gaining access to your facility as .00162, it is really more accurate to say that the intruder's chance of success is 'EXTREMELY LOW'. In making this replacement of 'EXTREMELY LOW' for .00162, we are sacrificing the "precision" of the numerical estimate to gain the believability and confidence of an inexact, "fuzzy" estimate that is both more realistic and easier to interpret.

These two limitations to risk analysis, overall complexity and inherent imprecision, can be overcome to some degree if one has access to an *automated* risk analysis utility that allows estimates of risk to be stated in *natural language terms* like 'VERY LOW,' 'MEDIUM TO HIGH,' or 'SOMEWHAT HIGH.' Both problems of overall complexity and inherent imprecision then become manageable. The automation present in this utility allows one to "simultaneously" consider a very large number of factors, something that would not be possible if you had to keep everything "in your head" or if you had to work by hand with the 2000 estimates for the risks associated with each of the 2000 components of the system. Thus, the apparent overall complexity of the risk analysis task is reduced to the job of estimating the risk of the individual components and then allowing the utility to combine these many estimates to produce the risk of the entire system. The other feature of the utility, that of accepting estimates in natural language terms, allows one to avoid the false precision that numerical estimates can provide, and it also allows one to form more reasonable estimates even with a paucity of data.

All of these benefits require that the automated risk analysis utility deal in an algorithmic fashion with natural language expressions in a way that is consistent with their use in ordinary discourse. This text describes such an automated risk analysis tool and provides the reader with the mathematical background necessary to understand the algorithms used to manipulate the natural language expressions. With this background and with the knowledge that psychological studies have demonstrated the "reasonableness" of this approach, the reader will then be prepared to knowledgeably use this automated risk analyzer.

Chapter 1

REVIEW OF SET THEORY

The theoretical foundations for the automated risk analysis utility that is to be described are in a rather specialized branch of modern mathematics: the theory of fuzzy sets. While one can study this theory at a very deep and mathematically sophisticated level, it is also possible to gain a great deal of useful insight at a more introductory and expository level. At this more elementary level, one can consider fuzzy set theory to be a generalization of ordinary set theory: the theory of collections of things. Much of the fundamentals of ordinary set theory are (or were!) the basis for the so-called "modern math" approach in elementary and secondary education and, therefore, are familiar to large numbers of people and can be grasped without much effort. For those who may have been away from such concepts for some time, as well as to gracefully ease into what will be for most a new topic, let us review some of the basic terms and ideas of ordinary set theory.

As is now known to most students of mathematics, one can consider the notion of a *set* as one of the most basic in modern mathematics. For our purposes we need only recall that a set is a collection of objects from some universe, U. If the universe is the natural numbers, we can form a set, A, composed of the numbers, 6, 222, and 376458. We would then write $A = \{6, 222, 376458\}$ and it would be exactly clear which numbers in the universe were in the set A (the *elements* of A) and which were not. When we specify a set by listing out all its elements as we did above for the set A, we have specified the set by *roster*. The only alternative is to specify the set by *rule*, i.e., to describe all its elements by some property or formula. A rule description of the set A would be the set of numbers that describe the length of this text in terms of the number of chapters, the number of pages, and the number of characters in the original manuscript. The rule method of specification is usually preferred in the case of infinite sets.

We could lump together the elements of two sets, taking their *union*, or we could examine the elements held in common by two sets, taking their *intersection*. We could also consider all the elements not in a set by taking its *complement*. It is assumed that the reader is quite familiar with such notions and with the conventional Venn diagrams for depicting these operations shown in Figure 1.1.

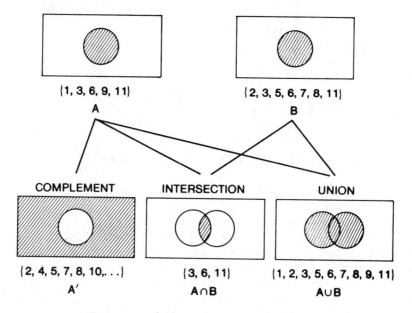

Figure 1.1   Set Union and Intersection.

One idea that may not be so familiar to the reader is a particularly precise specification for a set and the manner in which this specification can link set theory and logic. "It is common for logicians to give truth conditions for predicates in terms of classical set theory. 'John is tall' (or 'TALL(j)') is defined to be true just in case the individual denoted by 'John' (or 'j') is in the set of tall men" [Lakoff, 1973]. Hence, questions concerning logical reasoning can be reduced to a determination of set membership. The question of whether something is in a particular set can be answered through the use of a set specification method different from both the roster and the rule methods. We can, for any set, A, describe a function which determines for any element of the universe, whether that element is a member of A. Such a function is called the *characteristic function* of A, and is defined by:

$$char_A\,(x) = \begin{cases} 0 \text{ if } x \text{ is not in the set } A \\ 1 \text{ if } x \text{ is in the set } A \end{cases}$$

This function is defined for all the elements of the universe. It is a function mapping the whole of the universe U to the set of two elements $\{0, 1\}$. (We usually write this as $char_A\,(x): U \rightarrow \{0\ 1\}$.)

With an identification of $\{0, 1\}$ and $\{false, true\}$, this characteristic function can also play a role in assigning truth values to statements about A. The most elementary statement about A is one of the form "x is an element of A." In this case, the characteristic function also acts as a truth function: if x is an element of A, then $char_A(x) = 1 = true = $ truth_value ("x is an element of A").

These notions from set theory form the basis of modern mathematics, yet they seem rather inappropriate to our needs in risk analysis: they require too much precision - precision which we do not have and cannot obtain. It would also seem that any mathematical tools built upon this foundation would also inherit these deficiencies. We must use theories built on an entirely different base.

Chapter 2

FUZZY SET THEORY

With these preliminaries of set theory reviewed, let us propose a generalization of that theory. This generalization will be accomplished by suitably modifying the notion of *membership* in a set. What if an element was not completely *in* a set and was also not completely *out* of a set, but rather was half in and half out? Consider the following example:

$$A = \{x \mid x \text{ is a natural number and}$$
$$\text{Mary's car can hold } x \text{ adult passengers}\}$$

and suppose that Mary's car is a Pinto. Then it seems safe to state that 0, 1, 2, and 3 are all elements of A and it seems equally safe to state that 7, 8, 9, ... are not elements of A. But what about 4, 5, and 6? Intuitively, 4 is *more* in A than 6 is, or more precisely, it is more plausible that 4 is an element of A than it is that 6 is an element of A. This notion of the plausibility of set membership (as distinguished from the probability of set membership [Kaufmann, 1977], [Zadeh, 1980]) leads to the generalization of the *degree of membership* in a set, and from this generalization comes a variant of the set theory discussed earlier; this variant is called *fuzzy set theory*.

A fuzzy subset of some universe U is a collection of objects from U (the *set* part) such that with each object is associated a degree of membership (the *fuzzy* part). The degree of membership is always a real number between zero and one, and it measures the extent to which an element is in a fuzzy set, or in ordinary set-theoretic terms, it measures the plausibility of an element being in a particular set. A degree of membership of 0 for an element of a fuzzy set corresponds to an element that is not in an ordinary set, and a degree of membership of 1 corresponds to an element which is in an ordinary set. Therefore, if the universe is the set $\{a, b, c, d, e, f\}$, then a fuzzy subset, A, of this universe could be defined as

a is present with degree of membership 1.0
b is present with degree of membership .9
c is present with degree of membership .2

d is present with degree of membership .8
e is present with degree of membership 1.0
f is present with degree of membership 0

Equivalently, A could be written

$$\{1/a, .9/b, .2/c, .8/d, 1/e\}$$

where the degree of membership is juxtaposed next to each element and elements with 0 degree of membership are omitted.

The exact relationship of the notion of a fuzzy set to that of an ordinary set can be seen most clearly when one recalls the definition of the characteristic function of a set. For an ordinary set A, the characteristic function is of the form

$$char_A (x) : U \rightarrow \{0, 1\}$$

but for a fuzzy subset A, it is

$$char_A (x) : U \rightarrow [0, 1]$$

where here the degree of membership function is the characteristic function. The characteristic function of a fuzzy subset, instead of mapping to the set of two elements (a binary choice of either being in or out of a set), is a mapping to a portion of the real line, allowing a continuum of possible choices. If the range of the characteristic function of a fuzzy set, A, (i.e., its degree of membership function, $char_A (x)$: $U \rightarrow [0, 1]$), is in fact restricted to just the two values of 0 and 1, then this function reduces to an ordinary characteristic function and A reduces to an ordinary, non-fuzzy set. We see then that fuzzy set theory contains ordinary set theory as a special case.

Before we continue in our discussion of the principles of fuzzy sets and in the extension of results from ordinary set theory to fuzzy set theory, it is worthwhile to examine the motivation for making this extension. While it is certainly sufficient in this regard to say that fuzzy sets are studied for the same reason n-dimensional, non-Euclidean geometry or any other branch of higher mathematics is studied, because it is there, the manipulation of fuzzy sets represents something more than mental gymnastics. The originator of the notion of fuzzy sets, Lotfi A. Zadeh, has stated:

One of the aims of the theory of fuzzy sets is the development of a methodology for the formulation and solution of problems which are too complex or ill-defined to be susceptible to analysis by conventional techniques [Zadeh, 1980].

It is certainly true that risk analysis is both complex and ill-defined, so it would appear that this theory may be of interest and may provide an analytic tool for the analysis of risk that cannot be provided by the more traditional branches of mathematics. Thus, with our motivation newly refreshed, let us continue to explore this extension of ordinary set theory.

The universe from which a fuzzy set is constructed need not be finite. Consider the following fuzzy subset of the reals:

$$Y = \{m(x)/x \mid x \text{ is a positive real number}\}$$

where

$$m(x) = \begin{cases} 1.0 & \text{for } 0 < x \leq 25 \\ \left[1 + \left(\dfrac{x - 25}{5}\right)^2\right]^{-1} & \text{for } x > 25 \end{cases}$$

Such a set is often depicted graphically as shown in Figure 2.1.

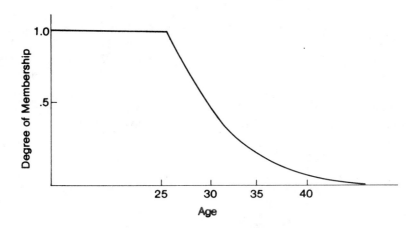

Figure 2.1   Degree of Membership.

The set Y can be thought of as a fuzzy set describing the imprecise term *young*—or more formally, as the set of ages of people who are young. Clearly someone under twenty-five is young, so the degree of membership of a number less than twenty-five is 1.0. It is not so clear that a person who is thirty is young,—so rather than saying that an individual 30-year-old is either young or not (only a binary choice), that individual can be said to be *partially* young (with a continuum of choices). This particular definition of the set *young* has a 30-year-old as half young and also approximates the degree of young-ness of a 40 year old as 0.1 (and appropriately so!). In this way, the imprecision connected with the concept of youth can be captured mathematically and dealt with in an algorithmic fashion. One might argue with the particular function used for the degree of membership function (especially if you are over forty), but this representation of the idea of *youth* will allow us to reason effectively using such an imprecise notion—a task not possible with the more traditional description of sets and of logical reasoning. (Later we will depict a finite fuzzy subset of a finite universe with such a graph as we used above for the set *young*. This is meant only as an aid to comprehension and to the building of intuition, not as a confusion between the finite and the infinite. The precise fuzzy set that is being used should always be clear from the context, regardless of the graphics used.)

The definition of basic operations on sets must also be modified for use in fuzzy set theory, and the most basic of these are *set union* and *set intersection*. It is not at all clear upon inspection how to extend these notions to the realm of fuzzy sets. If an object x has a degree of membership of .7 in the fuzzy set A, and a degree of membership of .3 in the fuzzy set B, what should its degree of membership be in the intersection of A and B? .3? .7? |.7−.3|?, max(.7, .3)?, min(.7, .3)?, (.7 + .3)/2? Which of these choices will yield a self-consistent theory and one that will assist us in the analysis of complex or ill-defined problems? The definition proposed by Zadeh was the following: if A and B are two fuzzy subsets of U and if $a(x)$ is the degree of membership of x in A and if $b(x)$ is the degree of membership of x in B then

$$A \cup B = \{max(\ a(x),\ b(x)\ )/x \mid x \text{ is an element of } U\}$$

and

$$A \cap B = \{min(\ a(x),\ b(x)\ )/x \mid x \text{ is an element of } U\}.$$

It has been shown that these definitions of the fuzzy union and the fuzzy intersetion are *the only* natural and reasonable definitions extending the standard set theory notion of union and intersection [Bellman and Giertz, 1973], [Yager, 1979]. These set operations have a very easily understood graphical representation, as shown in Figure 2.2. Note that there appears to be no exact analogy to the Venn diagrams used to depict traditional set union and intersection—the graphics of Figure 2.2 are the closest possible thing to a Venn diagram for fuzzy sets.

The only other set operation from traditional set theory that we will extend to fuzzy set theory in this text will be that of the complement of a set. The definition

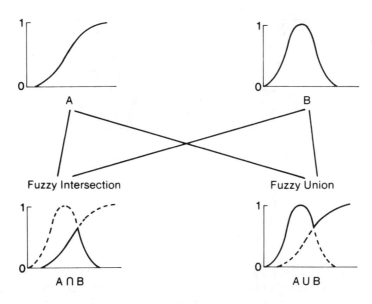

Figure 2.2 Fuzzy Union and Fuzzy Intersection.

proposed by Zadeh for the complement of a fuzzy set A (from a universe U) is

$$A' = \{ (1 - a(x))/x \mid x \text{ is in } U \}$$

This definition has the property that if the fuzzy set A reduces to an ordinary set (i.e., if it just so happens that the only degrees of membership for the elements of A are 0 and 1), then this definition of the complement and the traditional set theory definition yield identical results. This definition of the fuzzy complement is also very intuitive. After all, if an element is in a fuzzy set with plausibility .4, it seems quite reasonable (at first glance) that it should be present in the complement with degree .6. The graphical representation of fuzzy complement, shown in Figure 2.3, reflects and enforces this intuition. However, this intuitive feeling is challenged upon further reflection. The same type of proof that demonstrated that Zadeh's definition for fuzzy union and fuzzy intersection were the only natural and reasonable extensions possible from ordinary set theory has failed to demonstrate the corresponding result for the complement extension [Bellman and Giertz, 1973]. When one again considers the relationship between set theory and logic, the results become even more surprising.

As in ordinary set theory, the characteristic function of fuzzy sets links fuzzy set theory to fuzzy logic. The degree of membership of x in A corresponds to a "truth value" of the statement "x is a member of A." This correspondence has

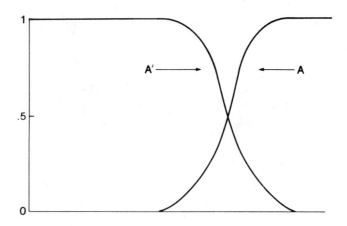

Figure 2.3   Fuzzy Complement.

profound (and sometimes puzzling) ramifications for "fuzzy logical reasoning."
If S and T are statements in such a fuzzy logic with truth values s and t,
respectively, then the truth value of the statement "S and T" has to be $min(s, t)$,
corresponding to definition of the fuzzy intersection. Let us consider the logical
counterpart to set complement: *negation*. If S is a statement in a fuzzy logic with
truth value s (and we can assume without loss of generality that $0 < s < .5$), then
the truth value of *not* S, using the correspondence with the set complement, is
$1 - s$. Consider now the fuzzy truth value of the statement "S and not S." Its truth
value must be $min(s, 1 - s) = s$. In fuzzy logic, the logical contradiction of "S and
not S" has a positive truth value! Indeed, one author stated

> In looking for natural restrictions on a function giving the truth value of "not S" in
> terms of that of S (in fuzzy logic), we must not be misled by the intuition the normal
> sharp mathematical use of "not" has given us. We might, for instance, be inclined to
> reject logically contradictory statements like "S and (not S)" completely. But in
> view of the definition of "and" in fuzzy set theory, this would force us to assign the
> truth value 0 to "not S" whenever the level of acceptance of S is positive, and this is
> clearly not what we want.
>   The reason that sentences rejected by ordinary logic may have a positive level of
> acceptance in fuzzy set theory is clear. In the latter context a positive acceptance of a
> statement S does not exclude the acceptance of its negation, and, therefore, not of
> the statement "S and (not S)" either. We may to some extent accept that a certain
> rose is red and at the same time not red. When we relax the rigid either-or condition
> of set theory the concept of negation necessarily becomes a fuzzy one. The border-
> line between S and "not S" is no longer sharp [Bellman and Giertz, 1973].

But for all its disturbing ramifications, Zadeh's definition of the complement still
"appears quite reasonable in practical applications" [Bellman and Giertz, 1973].

(It should be noted that some researchers are so perturbed by the "violation" of the tautologies of the propositional calculus (such as the tautology 'not(S and not S)' discussed above) that are exhibited when one makes the transition to fuzzy sets, that they have even proposed alternate definitions of fuzzy sets that do not disturb these basic truths [Schefe, 1980]!)

The fuzzy set operations presented so far are extensions of those from ordinary set theory. It is quite reasonable to expect that there will be important operations in fuzzy set theory that have no counterpart in ordinary set theory—operations that are uniquely fuzzy—and, in fact, this is the case.

We can *concentrate* the fuzzy elements of a set by reducing the degree of membership of all elements that are only "partly" in the set and in such a way that the less an element is in the set, the more we reduce its membership; we can stretch or *dilate* a fuzzy set by increasing the membership of elements that are only barely in the set; we can *normalize* a fuzzy set by adjusting the degree of membership of the elements so that at least one element is "totally" in the set; we can *intensify* a fuzzy set by increasing the degree of membership of all the elements that are at least half in the set and decreasing the degree of membership of the elements that are less than half in the set; we can also de-intensify or *fuzzify* a fuzzy set by increasing the extent of its fuzziness. These inherently fuzzy operations are defined below for the fuzzy set $A = \{a(x)/x \mid x$ is an element of $U\}$. Below each definition is a sketch of the effect of the transformation on the degree of membership function for A.

Concentration

$$CON(A) = \{a(x) \times a(x)/x \mid x \text{ is an element of } U\}$$

$$= \{a^2(x)/x \mid x \text{ is an element of } U\}$$

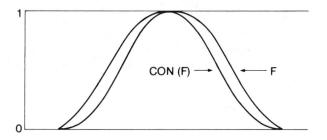

Since the degree of membership for any element of a fuzzy set is a real number between 0 and 1, the square of that degree of membership will also be between 0 and 1. We also have that if $x \in (0\ 1)$, then $x > x^2$, so, therefore, the *CON* operator decreases the degree of membership for all elements, except those with degrees of 0 or of 1. In addition, it has the property that it decreases the membership of elements that have low degrees of membership proportionally more than for elements with high degrees of membership. Consider that for an element x with degree of membership $a(x)$, the proportional decrease in the degree of membership under the *CON* operation is:

$$\frac{a(x) - a^2(x)}{a(x)} = 1 - a(x)$$

So for an element with degree of membership of .9, the proportional decrease of membership is .1, for an element with degree of membership of .4, it is .6, and for an element with only a .1 degree of membership, the proportional decrease is .9. In this way, the *CON* operator pulls a bell-shaped degree of membership graph (as pictured above) in toward the center and makes the graph more steep.

Dilation

$$DIL(A) = \{SQRT(a(x))/x \mid x \text{ is an element of } U\}$$

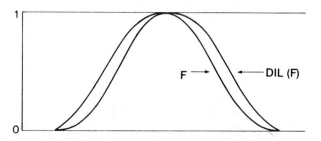

Dilation is the opposite of concentration. This operation modifies the graph of a bell-shaped degree of membership function (pictured above) by spreading it out more and making the slope less steep. Elements that are only just barely in the set (e.g., with a degree of membership of .01) increase their degree of membership tremendously (tenfold in the case of a .01 degree of membership). All this follows from the fact that the square root operation is the inverse of the square operation, which also implies that

$$A = CON(DIL(A)) = DIL(CON(A))$$

Normalization

$$NORM(A) = \{(a(x)/m)/x \mid x \text{ is an element of } U\}$$

where

$$m = \max_{x \in U} \{a(x)\}$$

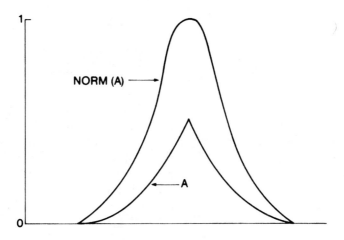

Normalization allows us to, in some sense, reduce all fuzzy sets to the same base. This is done in the same spirit in which vectors in linear algebra are normalized to unit vectors. (For example, the two-dimensional vectors (1,2) and (4,8) both normalize to $(1/\sqrt{5}, 2/\sqrt{5})$ and, thus, we are able to show that both these vectors have the same direction.) Normalization insures us that at least one element of the set has a degree of membership of one. This is done by dividing the degree of membership of each element in the set by the maximum degree of membership of any element in the set. If this maximum degree of membership is one, then the set is not modified by this division. If, on the other hand, the maximum degree of membership in the set is a number less than one, then dividing by this maximum will increase the degree of membership of each element, and at least one element (one of the elements with that maximum degree of membership) will have a degree of membership of one after the division.

Intensification

$$INT(A) = \{m(x)/x \mid x \text{ is an element of } U\}$$

$$m(x) = \begin{cases} 2a^2(x) & \text{for } 0 \leq a(x) \leq 0.5 \\ 1 - 2[1 - a(x)]^2 & \text{for } 0.5 < a(x) \leq 1.0 \end{cases}$$

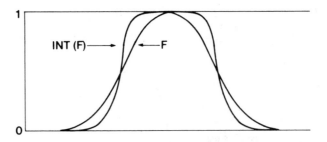

Intensification acts like a combination of concentration and dilation—it raises the degree of membership of some elements, lowers some others, and modifies the steepness of the degree of membership curve. Since intensification increases the degree of membership only for the elements that have a degree of membership greater than .5, and since it lowers the degree of membership of elements whose degree of membership is less than .5, intensification heightens the contrast between the elements that are more than half in the set and those that are less then half in.

Fuzzification

$$\text{Fuzzification of } A = \bigcup \{a(x)*K(x)\}$$

where K maps elements of U into fuzzy subsets of U, * is an extension of ordinary multiplication to the multiplication of a fuzzy set by a real number, and $\bigcup$ is the fuzzy union discussed earlier. An example (from [Zadeh, 1972A]) may clarify this operation. Let

$$U = \{1, 2, 3, 4\}$$
$$A = \{.8/1, .6/2\}$$
$$K(1) = \{1/1, .4/2\}$$
$$K(2) = \{.4/1, 1/2, .4/3\}$$

Fuzzification of $A =$

$$= .8\ K(1)\ \cup\ .6\ K(2)$$
$$= .8\ \{1/1,\ .4/2\}\ \cup\ .6\ \{.4/1,\ 1/2,\ .4/3\}$$
$$= \{.8/1,\ .32/2\}\ \cup\ \{.24/1,\ .6/2,\ .24/3\}$$
$$= \{.8/1,\ .6/2,\ .24/3\}$$

What we are doing in this operation is to *fuzzify* each element of a particular fuzzy set, e.g., the element 1 is mapped into 1 (with degree of membership 1) and 2 (with degree of membership .4); (this is the $K(1)$ above—it is the fuzzification of the element 1); the element 2 is mapped into 1 (with degree of membership .4), 2 (with degree of membership 1), and 3 (with degree of membership .4). (This is $K(2)$.) This operation is heavily dependent on the choice of the function K and, to denote this dependence, the operation is normally written $SF(A;K)$ (read the support fuzzification of A with respect to K). It is unfortunately rather difficult to graph the results of this operation, as we have done for concentration, dilation, normalization, and intensification, so it is not attempted here for the general set A. For the case of the "fuzzy" singleton set $\{1/5\}$, we can provide a semi-satisfactory graphical representation of the fuzzy operation $SF(\{1/5\}, K)$ where

$$K(5) = \{.50/3,\ .8/4,\ 1/5,\ .8/6,\ .50/7\}.$$

The graphical representation of this fuzzy operation is shown in Figure 2.4.

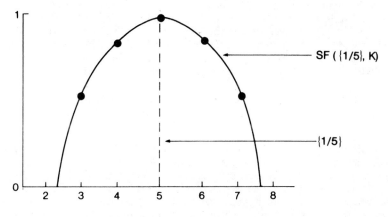

Figure 2.4 Fuzzification.

We see that the operation of fuzziness has enlarged the set of elements with non-zero degrees of membership—the so-called "support" of a fuzzy set, hence, the term "support fuzzification."

More specifically, the support fuzzification spreads the degree of membership of individual elements of a fuzzy set to a (possibly) large number of elements (its support). In the example given above, the fuzzy set $K(5)$ is the support for the element 5 and since 5 is the only element with a non-zero degree of membership, only $K(5)$ is important to the support fuzzification of $\{1/5\}$. The definition of any other $K(i)$, $i \neq 5$, is irrelevant in this particular example.

This concludes our excursion into fuzzy set *theory*. Henceforth, we will be concerned with the application of that theory in the area of risk analysis. However, before we focus completely on risk analysis, we would be remiss in our obligations, especially to the non-mathematically inclined reader, if we did not attempt to convey the breadth of other applications of fuzzy set theory as well as the enthusiasm and fervor of both theoretical and applied fuzzy researchers. One such researcher conveyed this very well:

> It is my belief that in systems theory, in the theory of languages, in all that is concerned with automata and Turing machines, in machines with parallel processing as in Rosenblatt's perceptrons, in such abstract areas as topology as well as in the much more concrete areas relating to pattern recognition, in quantum physics and geophysics, and in many other areas too numerous to cite, the theory of fuzzy subsets offers new and powerful tools for analysis, synthesis, and systematic study. Its influence in science has been felt already and is certain to grow in the years to come.
>
> Like others, I have encountered antagonistic attitudes toward the theory of fuzzy subsets, but it did not take me long to realize that such attitudes were a reflection of prior prejudice, professed by those who did not want or did not have the time to study the theory or its ramifications. But I have yet to meet anyone who remained opposed to the theory of fuzzy subsets after becoming familiar with its substance. Needless to say, whatever can be explained by the theory of fuzzy subsets can also be explained in other ways. But is this not also true of all mathematical theories? The *raison d'etre* for mathematics is its power and fertility. The same can be said about the theory of fuzzy subsets, a part of modern mathematics [Kaufmann, 1977].

Zadeh has very often expressed his belief in the pervasiveness and breadth of fuzziness:

> Thus, the pervasiveness of fuzziness derives from the fact that, in most of the classes of objects that we form in our perception of reality, the transition from membership to nonmembership is gradual rather than abrupt. This is true of the classes of tall men, beautiful women, and large numbers. And it is true of the meanings of such concepts as meaning, intelligence, truth, democracy, and love. In fact, the only domain of human knowledge in which non-fuzzy concepts play the dominant role is that of classical mathematics. On the one hand, this endows mathematics with a beauty, power, and universality unmatched by any other field. On the other hand, it severely restricts its applicability in fields in which fuzziness is pervasive—as is true, in particular, of humanistic systems, that is, systems in which human judgement, perception, and emotions play a central role [Zadeh, 1977B].

For our purposes, the uniquely fuzzy operations we have explained above, of concentration, dilation, normalization, intensification, and fuzzification are more than just new types of set operations made possible by the extension of traditional sets to fuzzy sets. These operations also have analogs in "fuzzy" logic," in the same way that, for example, logical negation is analogous to set complement. This correspondence to fuzzy logic will enable us to mathematically model and solve natural language logical arguments like the following (taken from [Zadeh, 1980]):

X is a large number.
Y is much larger than X.

How large is Y?

Mike is much taller than most of his close friends.

How tall is Mike?

It is for such modeling, or more precisely for the modeling of vague and approximate English expressions, that we have made the considerable intellectual investment of mastering fuzzy set theory. We shall make use of that investment in the next section when we use fuzzy sets to model natural language estimates of risk.

Chapter 3

NATURAL LANGUAGE
COMPUTATION

There is, almost at the very core of the Western view of scientific knowledge, an affinity for precise quantification, for numbers and for the precision they seem to imply. The roots of this veneration of numbers are quite deep—one can find their beginnings in the statements of such pioneers as Lord Kelvin, who in 1883 stated:

> In physical science a first essential step in the direction of learning any subject is to find principles of numerical reckoning and practicable methods for measuring some quality connected with it. I often say that when you can measure what you are speaking about and express it in numbers, you know something about it; but when you cannot measure it, when you cannot express it in numbers, your knowledge is of a meager and unsatisfactory kind: it may be the beginning of knowledge but you have scarcely, in your thoughts, advanced to the state of *science*, whatever the matter may be. (Quotation from *Popular Lectures and Addresses*, Sir William Thomson, McMillian, London, 1891)

So deep are these roots that they have almost become inborn intuition to the modern researcher—an intuition that may now be modified because of the wide spread availability of computer power.

The advent of the computer did little, at first, to affect this intuitive feeling. This is because in the early days of the computer, computers were extremely expensive, difficult to program and to use, and very limited in power and scope. White-robed priests attended to them and prepared their input with great attention to the form most easily assimilated by the machine and with little thought for the convenience of the human users. Because the computer had been designed to process numbers, the early computers were naturally put to highly numerical tasks—ballistic computations, actuarial table preparation, and statistical calculations, to name a few. There were some people, however, who were able to see beyond these uses of the computer—beyond the so-called "number crunching" tasks—and to envision the flexibility of the computer applied to other types of tasks, tasks that were less numerical and less precise (at least to the extent that numbers and precision are synonymous). For example, as early as 1946 the use of computers for the translation of one natural language to another was proposed. The task of translating, like many other tasks, is inherently different from that of, say, a ballistic calculation—in these different tasks there is no one right answer, but rather degrees of correctness. Humans performing these types of tasks vary in their degree of expertness—in translation this can include as wide a range as from the college student with a smattering of Spanish to the professional polyglot who is fluent in several languages. Such tasks, unlike their numerical counterparts, are extremely difficult to program—indeed, the machine translation problem has yet to be solved, except for a few very restricted areas, despite the four decades of work. But one successful notion that has emerged from this period of work in machine translation (and other areas) is that of *computer assistance*, i.e., in these types of tasks, the computer is often best used as an analytic aid—assisting the human in his nebulous task. One such nebulous task is the analysis of risk.

Risk analysis is a task without a clearly discernible measure of success; it involves "best guesses," intuition, and straw man estimates. Often, because of manpower limitations, preliminary risk evaluations must be made by other than well-trained professionals with extensive backgrounds. In these circumstances it seems ludicrous for an inexperienced risk analyst to estimate that some particular component will fail 7.327 times per year. People rarely have the data to prepare such precise estimates and, in many cases when there is a wealth of data, the precision is false. Even if one has, for example, the records on every case of privacy violation involving a particular computer, this data is of little use in predicting the extent or the frequency of future violations - there are just too many uncontrollable variables. In addition, categorizations such as "This is a privacy violation and this is not" are not easily made—throwing doubt upon the validity of the data itself. One of the first researchers in this area has stated:

> ...a purely numerically-based rating system demands a degree of precision on the part of the system rater which is both difficult to attain and difficult to interpret with confidence. ... Conceptualizing a .65 secure system is much more difficult than visualizing, say, a .65 full cup of coffee. The latter concept is tough enough as it is [Clements, 1977].

The theory of fuzzy sets offers a natural model for such a situation. In fact, one author has stated that fuzzy set theory

> is an attempt to remove "linguistic" barriers between humans, who think in fuzzy terms, and machines that accept only precise instructions [Gupta, 1977].

The very core of fuzzy set theory (as we have seen) models an imprecise situation like the estimation of risk by allowing one to estimate the plausibility or the possibility of an element being a member of a set. However, the theory can be difficult to use directly—especially difficult for a novice. Fortunately, a *linguistic variable*—a notion built on top of fuzzy set theory—offers a viable alternative. The use of such a linguistic variable allows a precise modeling of imprecise statements like 'LOW', 'SOMEWHAT LOW', and 'VERY LOW TO FAIRLY LOW'. Linguistic variables allow for the easy and natural specification of values for imprecise concepts—a specification that has a firm theoretical base for computations that can be performed behind the scenes. Such behind-the-scenes computations can provide users with, for example, a reliable, consistent way of assessing the overall risk of a complex system.

The notions of linguistic variables and of fuzzy sets are not one and the same but rather have the relationship of goal and tool: having precisely manipulatable natural language expressions is the goal, and fuzzy set theory is a tool to achieve that goal. While fuzzy set theory (and in particular its use to provide us with linguistic variables) is relatively new, the goal of having something like a linguistic variable is rather old. Leibnitz, the co-inventor of the calculus with Isaac Newton, once expressed it:

> if we could find characters or signs appropriate for expressing all our thoughts as definitely and as exactly as arithmetic expresses numbers or geometric analysis expresses lines, we could in all subjects, in so far as they are amenable to reasoning, accomplish what is done in arithmetic and geometry.

Having now put ourselves in the noble company of Liebnitz and alined our goals with his, we begin our discussion of how to obtain that goal: with a fuzzy set model of natural language expressions—the linguistic variable.

A linguistic variable is a variable whose values are natural language expressions referring to some quantity of interest. These natural language expressions are then, in turn, names for fuzzy sets composed of the possible numerical values that the quantity of interest can assume. (In this particular case of linguistic variables, these fuzzy sets are sometimes referred to as fuzzy restrictions for reasons that will be clear momentarily.) Figure 3.1 diagrams this relationship for the case where the quantity of interest is the risk of fire. (See Appendix A for a formal definition of a linguistic variable.)

> A linguistic variable differs from a numerical variable in that its values are not numbers but words or sentences in a natural or artificial language. Since words, in general, are less precise than numbers, the concept of a linguistic variable serves the purpose of providing a means of approximate characterization of phenomena which are too complex or too ill-defined to be amenable to description in conventional quantitative terms. More specifically, the fuzzy sets which represent the restriction associated with the values of a linguistic variable may be viewed as summaries of various subclasses of elements in a universe of discourse. This, of course, is analogous to the role played by words and sentences in a natural language. For example, the adjective *handsome* is a summary of a complex of

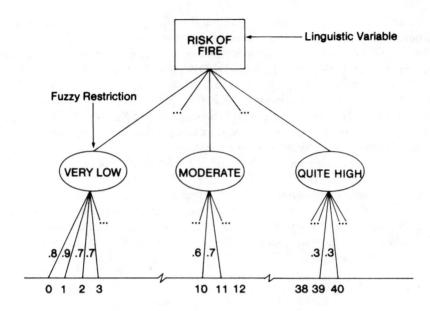

Figure 3.1 Schematic of a Linguistic Variable.

characteristics of the appearance of an individual. It may also be viewed as a label for a fuzzy set which represents a restriction imposed by a fuzzy variable named *handsome*. From this point of view, then, the terms *very handsome, not handsome, extremely handsome, quite handsome*, etc., are names of fuzzy sets which result from operating on the fuzzy set named *handsome* with the modifiers named *very, not, extremely, quite*, etc. In effect, these fuzzy sets, together with the fuzzy set labeled *handsome*, play the role of values of the linguistic variable *Appearance* [Zadeh, 1975].

A detailed, small example of a linguistic variable may demonstrate its structure. Let us define one named *Number*. The quantity of interest will just be an integer between 1 and 10. The set of natural language expressions that *Number* can take as its values is {'few', 'several', 'many'}. These in turn are names of the following fuzzy sets:

$$\text{'few'} = \{.4/1, .8/2, 1/3, .4/4\}$$
$$\text{'several'} = \{.5/3, .8/4, 1/5, 1/6, .8/7, .5/8\}$$
$$\text{'many'} = \{.4/6, .6/7, .8/8, .9/9, 1/10\}$$

The pictorial representation for the linguistic variable *Number* is shown in Figure 3.2.

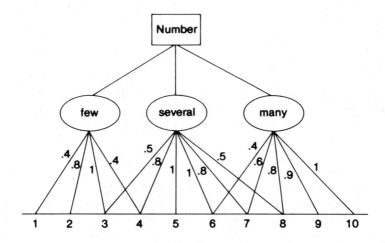

Figure 3.2 The Linguistic Variable 'Number'.

The set of natural language expressions in which the linguistic variable takes its values is not an unrestricted set of English phrases. Rather it is a (hopefully) rich finite set that is carefully structured by the system designer. Because the set is often quite large, it is usually not specified by roster, but rather by rule. The most natural form of the rule is that of a Phrase-Structure grammar, or, using a slightly more restricted form better known to computer scientists, the set of possible natural language values for a linguistic variable can be specified using Backus-Naur Form (BNF). Figure 3.3 shows a small set of such rules (taken, with slight modifications, from Hoffman and Neitzel [1980]). The terms <Hedge>, <Primary>, <Fuzzifier>, etc. (the non-terminals of the grammar) play the roles that 'subject', 'verb', 'object', etc., do in the construction of sets of English sentences, i.e., they are the building blocks used to construct the elements of the set. Of these, the *primary terms* and the *hedges* are the most important. Just as 'subjects' and 'verbs' have certain roles to fill in the construction of English sentences, so too the primary terms and hedges fulfill certain functional roles in

<Rating> ::= (<Hedged Primary> | <Range Phrase>) − <Confidence>
<Confidence> ::= <Fuzzifier> CONFIDENT
<Range Phrase> ::= <Hedged Primary> TO <Hedged Primary>
<Hedged Primary > ::= <Hedged> <Primary> | <Primary>
<Hedge> ::= NOT | VERY | FAIRLY | SLIGHTLY
<Primary> ::= LOW | HIGH | MEDIUM
<Fuzzifier> ::= REASONABLY | BARELY | null

Figure 3.3 BNF Notation for a Simple Set of Natural Language Expressions.

the construction of the set of possible natural language expressions that a linguistic variable can assume as its values. The primary terms are the fundamental notions from which all the other elements of the set are built and the hedges allow for the fine tuning of these primary terms. For example, if the vulnerability of your system's physical security safeguards is low, but you know of several common conditions that could undermine those safeguards, you might not rate the system risk to physical threats as 'LOW' but rather as 'MORE OR LESS LOW'. The hedge, 'MORE OR LESS', reflects your dissatisfaction with the current safeguards and is a modification of the basic feeling that the system risk is low.

It is the goal of the system designer of an automated risk analysis facility to (1) have a sufficiently rich set of primary terms and hedges so that the user feels almost unrestricted in his range of expression and (2) to associate with each possible natural language expression that can be generated by these rules a technical, precise meaning that is consistent with the imprecise, nebulous English meaning. (As the designer of any system of any reasonable size knows, these conditions are impossible to realize! Nothing is ever sufficient and no matter what you do, someone will think it is unnatural and contrived. Such is the cross that system designers bear.) In *attempting* to satisfy these conditions, the system designer has three degrees of freedom: He selects the *primitives*, the *hedges*, and the *possible ranges* as well as their exact technical definitions.

There is in risk analysis, unfortunately, almost no flexibility possibe in the choices of the actual terms used for the primitives (LOW, MEDIUM, and HIGH are pretty standard) or the range (What could it be except TO?); there is, however, much freedom in the meanings to be attached to these terms inside the system. The hedges allow the system designer an even greater wealth of possible choices for the actual terms and an accompanying bevy of choices and special problems in the precise meanings to be given to those hedges. Figure 3.4 (taken from Clements, 1977) shows a more complete set of rules that generate a much larger, more complex set of natural language expressions. The rules of Figure 3.4 generate a more complex set containing the following expressions (in addition to many others):

HIGH	LOW
MEDIUM	NOT HIGH
MORE OR LESS HIGH	MEDIUM TO SORT OF HIGH
INDEED LOW	SLIGHTLY LOWER THAN PRETTY HIGH
ABOUT FOUR TO ABOUT SIX	NOT HIGHER THAN MEDIUM
HIGHER THAN LOW AND LOWER THAN SORT OF HIGH	

(Even this very complex set of rules isn't completely satisfactory—what intuitive meaning is assigned to 'FAIRLY PRETTY HIGH', or to 'SLIGHTLY LOWER THAN NOT MEDIUM', two other expressions generated by these rules?)

<sentence> ::= <compound phrase> | <simple phrase>
<compound phrase> ::= <conjunctive phrase> | <range phrase>
<simple phrase> ::= <relational phrase> | <hedged primary>
<conjunctive phrase> ::= <relational phrase> AND <relational phrase>
<range phrase> ::= <hedged primary> TO <hedged primary>
<relational phrase> ::= <composite relation> THAN <hedged primary>
<composite relation> ::= <relation hedge> <relation> | <relation>
<relation hedge> ::= NOT | MUCH | SLIGHTLY
<relation> ::= LOWER | HIGHER
<hedged primary> ::= <hedge> <primary> | <primary> | <fuzzy number>
<hedge> ::= NOT | VERY | MORE OR LESS | FAIRLY | PRETTY | SORT OF|
            EXTREMELY | INDEED | REALLY
<primary> ::= LOW | HIGH | MEDIUM
<fuzzy number> ::= <fuzzifier> <number>
<fuzzifier> ::= ABOUT
<number> ::= ONE | TWO | THREE | FOUR | FIVE | SIX | SEVEN | EIGHT | NINE

Figure 3.4 More Complex BNF for a Set of Natural Language Expressions.

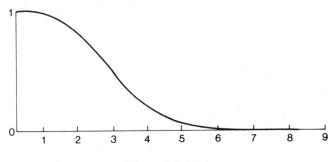

Figure 3.5 Low.

The assignment of meaning to the primary terms is the assignment of a fuzzy restriction to each one of these terms. Suppose, for the moment, that the universe is the set of positive integers from 1 to 9. Then one possible fuzzy restriction that can be assigned to LOW is

$$\{1/1, .85/2, .53/3, .24/4, .08/5, .02/6\}$$

which is shown graphically in Figure 3.5. The other primary terms, MEDIUM and HIGH, can be given other appropriately similar definitions. It cannot be overemphasized that these definitions are subjective, somewhat arbitrary choices made by the system designers *a priori*. It is hoped that these definitions correspond in some way with the user's intuitive meanings for the terms 'low', 'high', and 'medium' and more will be said later about demonstrations of the correlation between these fuzzy definitions and intuition. Note that because these fuzzy restrictions assigned to the natural language expressions are so arbitrary, the ability to re-define the meanings assigned to these primitives is an extremely powerful capability that the designer of an automated version of a linguistic variable could choose to implement. Such a capability would allow the system to be fine-tuned to each installation, to each set of users, to each application domain, etc. Such a capability presents several difficult problems for the system designer. Some of these will be discussed later.

The *hedges* are not themselves modeled by fuzzy sets as the primary terms are, but rather are modeled as operators on the fuzzy restrictions that represents the primary terms. For example, in everyday English the hedge 'very' intensifies the particular word it modifies. An implementation or modeling of this hedge should then decrease the fuzziness of the elements of the fuzzy set that models the modified word. That is, the implementation of 'VERY' should "remove" the elements that are only "part of the way" in the set, i.e., it should decrease the degree of membership for elements whose degree of membership is less than one. The concentration operator, *CON*, discussed earlier performs this function and one reasonable implementation of the hedge 'VERY' is based on this operator. Specifically,

> VERY LOW = *CON*(low)
> > where 'low' is the fuzzy restriction we have chosen for the primitive LOW.

Similarly, we can define other hedges acting on a fuzzy restriction as follows. For the moment we will let 'term' represent the fuzzy restriction, $\{t(x)/x \mid x$ is an element of the universe\}, that models a given primary term, prim_term. Then some accepted "meanings" for some commonly used hedges are:

> NOT prim_term = term'
> > = \{ $(1-t(x))/x \mid x$ is an element of the universe\}
>
> MORE OR LESS prim_term = SF(term, k)
> SORT OF prim_term = NORM(INT(DIL(term)) AND INT (DIL(term')))
> PRETTY prim_term = NORM(INT(term) AND (INT(CON(term))) ')
> RATHER prim_term = NORM(INT(CON(term) AND (CON(term))'))
> SLIGHTLY prim_term = NORM(term AND NOT VERY prim_term)

where AND is modeled by the fuzzy set intersection operator discussed earlier. Figures 3.6 and 3.7 depict the effects of these hedges. (Figure 3.6 is taken from Lakoff [1973] and Figure 3.7 from Zadeh [1972].)

It cannot be overemphasized that these definitions are biased decisions of the system designer. While it is hoped that they reflect the normal meanings given to

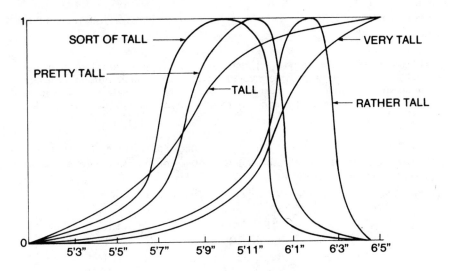

Figure 3.6 Hedges Acting on 'TALL'.

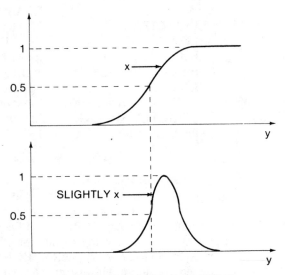

Figure 3.7 The Hedge 'SLIGHTLY'.

the English terms they represent, there is much room here for disagreement. Even Zadeh states that:

> It should be emphasized, however, that these representations are intended mainly to illustrate the approach rather than to provide accurate definitions of the hedges in question. Furthermore it must be underscored that our analysis and its conclusions are tentative in nature and may require modification in later work [Zadeh, 1972].

The set of hedges that the system designer has to pick from (if he can figure out how to model them satisfactorily!) is almost endless. Some that have been suggested are listed in Figure 3.8. These are taken from a variety of sources [Clements, 1977], [Lakoff, 1973], [Zadeh, 1972], and [Zadeh, 1975].

ESSENTIALLY	VIRTUALLY	VERY
SORT OF	RATHER	NOT
TECHNICALLY	ALMOST	MUCH
KIND OF	REGULAR	FAIRLY
ACTUALLY	MOSTLY	PRETTY
LOOSELY SPEAKING	IN ESSENCE	BARELY
STRICTLY	BASICALLY	REASONABLY
ROUGHLY	PRINCIPALLY	EXTREMELY
IN A SENSE	LOWER THAN	INDEED
RELATIVELY	HIGHER THAN	REALLY
PRACTICALLY	PARTICULARLY	MORE OR LESS
SOMEWHAT	LARGELY	PSEUDO-
EXCEPTIONALLY	FOR THE MOST PART	NOMINALLY
ANYTHING BUT	STRICTLY SPEAKING	LITERALLY
OFTEN	ESPECIALLY	TYPICALLY
DAMN		

Figure 3.8 Some Possible Hedges.

Representing hedges as operators acting upon the representation of the primary terms has both positive and negative implications. On the positive side, it seems very natural and also allows for an easy implementation of the concatenation of several hedges. An expression like 'NOT VERY HIGH' can be represented by the fuzzy set obtained as follows: The operator *CON* is applied to the fuzzy restriction for HIGH, and then the operator NOT is applied to that result. Mathematically, we are determining the operator that represents a group of several hedges by the *functional composition* of the operators for the individual hedges. This has the advantages of ease of implementation and theoretical simplicity. For example, 'VERY VERY LOW' can be represented by *CON*

(CON(low)). This use of function composition automatically makes the expressions 'NOT VERY HIGH' and 'VERY NOT HIGH' different. The first is represented by not (CON(high)) and the second by CON(not(high)). These are not the same fuzzy restriction and this is just what is desired from a thoughtful examination of the intuitive meanings of each natural language expression.

The negative side of representing hedges as operators is that some hedges don't seem to be easily modeled by such an approach. By this we mean that the way people normally use these hedges entails an implementation considerably different and more complex than than of an operator that acts uniformly upon the fuzzy restrictions that represent the various primary terms. Zadeh differentiates four types of hedges, only *one* of which can be implemented as an operator of the type we have shown above [Zadeh, 1972]. An examination of the way people use the hedges 'regular', 'technically', and 'strictly speaking', in ordinary prose will show some extent of this complexity

Consider the following two sentences:

a) His daughter is a monkey.

b) His daughter is a regular monkey.

If we assume that it is a *person* being discussed (either parent or offspring!), then clearly (a) is a false statement. The second statement, (b), could be true, assuming that the child involved climbs all over things, is mischievous, eats bananas, etc. Note that (b) does not assert that the child being discussed has a tail and drags her knuckles along the ground. In fact, (b) presupposes that the child is not literally a monkey, but rather that she has certain monkey-like characteristics. Hence, we see that the hedge 'regular' can imply a negation of the literal meaning of the word it modifies, while asserting *some* of that word's connotations.

The hedges 'technically' and 'strictly speaking' seem to operate just the opposite of the hedge 'regular'. Consider the following three sentences:

The tomato is a fruit.

The tomato is technically a fruit.

Strictly speaking, the tomato is a fruit.

Here we see that 'technically' and 'strictly speaking' take on sort of a "despite-the-common-impression" meaning, and apply a strict adherence to the technical definition. However, the matter is not as simple as this last example would lead us to believe. An example from Lakoff, [1973] demonstrates the subtle distinction between these two superficially similar hedges:

Richard Nixon is technically a Quaker.

Strictly speaking, Richard Nixon is a Quaker.

As this example shows, *technically* picks out some definitional criterion, while *strictly speaking* requires both the definitional criterion and other important criteria as well. Richard Nixon may be a Quaker in some definitional sense, but he does not have the religious and ethical views characteristic of Quakers. He meets the definitional criterion but not the other important criteria.

There is much fundamental and basic work in the linguistic subspecialties of both semantics and pragmatics that must be done before the full range of English hedges can be understood to the point that they can be easily modeled for use in a computer input method like the one we are proposing. For the time being, we will have to be content with a much smaller set.

Once meanings have been assigned to both the primary terms and to the hedges (the primary terms receiving a particular fuzzy set as a meaning; the hedges receiving an operator on fuzzy sets as a meaning), one must assign meanings to the combinations of hedged primary terms. There are two cases of such combinations. The first case is in the formation of natural language expressions with a *range*, as in 'VERY LOW *TO* FAIRLY HIGH' and 'MEDIUM *TO* MORE OR LESS HIGH'. The other case is the combination of a number of hedged primary terms (or even ranged expressions) in the ultimate computation of the risk for some system. This second combination involves the weighted averaging of a number of fuzzy restrictions, and as such its discussion will be postponed until the next section which deals with the inner workings of the Fuzzy Risk Analyzer, an actual implementation of the ideas presented in this text.

Meanings for the ranged natural language expressions are constructed by operating on the meanings of the two components of the range. The operation is the fuzzy union discussed earlier, possibly with some "adjusting" of the resulting fuzzy set. Figure 3.9 shows the construction of the meaning of the expression 'MORE OR LESS LOW TO MEDIUM'. (Strictly speaking, the phrase 'MORE OR LESS LOW TO MEDIUM' is ambiguous. It can be interpreted as the hedge 'MORE OR LESS' applied to the ranged expression 'LOW TO MEDIUM' or it can be interpreted as the ranged expression of 'MORE OR LESS LOW' and 'MEDIUM'. In our explanation of the construction of the fuzzy meaning for such expressions, only the second is possible since hedges are applied only to primary terms.) The fuzzy union is taken of the fuzzy sets representing 'MEDIUM' and the fuzzy set resulting from applying the more-or-less operator to the fuzzy set representing 'LOW'. The adjustment that is normally made to the resulting fuzzy set is to insure its convexity. Keeping all fuzzy sets convex makes the job of later finding a natural language expression to describe a computed fuzzy set easier, and some authors [Clements, 1977] find convex fuzzy sets more

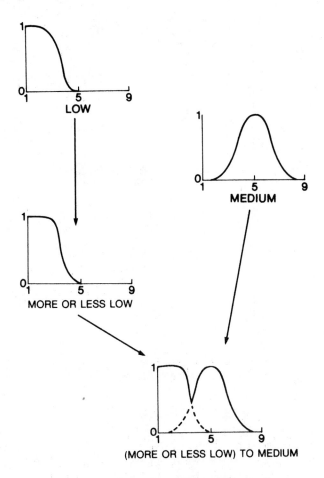

LOW

MEDIUM

MORE OR LESS LOW

(MORE OR LESS LOW) TO MEDIUM

Figure 3.9   Construction of Ranged Expressions.

intuitive representations for natural language expressions. Whatever the reason, Figure 3.10 shows the result of the convexity operation on the fuzzy set derived in Figure 3.9. We shall take the meaning of a ranged phrase 'X to Y' as

$$\text{Meaning } (X \text{ TO } Y) = \text{Convex(Meaning}(X) \cup \text{Meaning}(Y))$$

One other adjustment that is often made to a fuzzy set representing a natural language expression is normalization. The same justification given above for requiring convexity is also usually given for requiring normalization. (This rationale may not be sufficient—see the chapter on Future Research.)

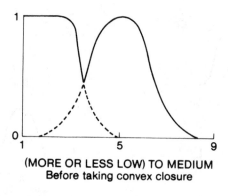

(MORE OR LESS LOW) TO MEDIUM
Before taking convex closure

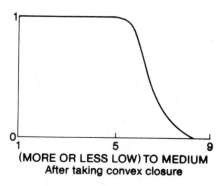

(MORE OR LESS LOW) TO MEDIUM
After taking convex closure

Figure 3.10   Convexity.

At this point we can construct a fuzzy set meaning for a wide range of natural language expressions, and we have alluded to the fact that we will use these fuzzy sets in a series of yet unspecified computations to determine the overall risk of a system being analyzed. At that point, we meet the problem of describing the resulting fuzzy set with a suitable natural language expression from our rating language. This problem is by no means a simple or easy one to solve. While the details have not yet been explained to the reader, the computation that will calculate the overall risk of a system *will not* (in general) yield a fuzzy set that exactly corresponds to one of the natural language expressions generated by the grammar we have chosen to describe the primary terms and hedges. This is not unlike the problem of averaging the set of integers 1, 2, and 5 *and being forced to "describe" the average as an integer*! Do you round up, round down, truncate, or what? For fuzzy averaging, the problems are even more complex.

Here we must digress momentarily and discuss proper terminology: some authors describe this operation of finding an appropriate natural language expression for a given fuzzy set as "translating back into linguistics"—a totally meaningless expression. While undoubtedly this phrase has its origins in Zadeh's "linguistic variable" and "linguistic approximation" phrases, these writers use much less precision than Zadeh. The Oxford English Dictionary defines linguistics as "the science of languages" or "pertaining to the knowledge or the study of languages." Thus, language is to liguistics as, say, blood is to hematology. To talk of translating back into linguistics is as meaningful as ordering a pint of O-negative hematology! The reader venturing forward into the literature of fuzzy sets is, therefore, forewarned to expect a certain amount of license with respect to the terms 'linguistics' and 'language.' One might say that the sharp distinction between language and linguistics is seen as a fuzzy boundary (or even a non-existent one) by some authors!

This problem of "translating back to linguistics" is an exceptionally difficult one for which solutions at various levels of sophistication exist. We will assume only that the fuzzy set for which a natural language expression is desired is both normalized and convex and in our later examples we will enforce our normality and convexity conditions on all fuzzy sets, even those involved in intermediate calculations. Given these conditions we shall discuss three techniques for this mapping: Best Fit, Successive Approximation, and Piecewise Decomposition. The Best Fit method is usually employed when the set of possible natural language expressions is small, as is the case with the set generated by the BNF in Figure 3.3. In this case, one just calculates the Euclidean distance from the given fuzzy set to each of the fuzzy sets representing each of the possible natural language expressions. For example, if all the fuzzy sets concerned are defined on the universe consisting of the integers from 1 to 9 inclusive, and if Z is the fuzzy set for which we are to find a natural language approximation, and A is a fuzzy set representing one of the natural language expressions in the rating language, then the "distance" between Z and A can be calculated as follows:

$$Z = \{z(i)/i \mid i \text{ is an element of the universe}\}$$
$$= \{z(1)/1, z(2)/2, z(3)/3, z(4)/4, z(5)/5,$$
$$z(6)/6, z(7)/7, z(8)/8, z(9)/9\}$$

$$A = \{a(i)/i \mid i \text{ is an element of the universe}\}$$

$$\text{distance}(Z,A) = \left[\sum_{i=1}^{9} (z(i) - a(i))^2 \right]^{1/2}$$

We then perform this calculation for all of the natural language expressions in the rating language. The natural language expression that is the shortest distance from Z is taken to be the best fit to Z and is used as its natural language equivalent. While one might not be attracted to this Best Fit method on the grounds of theoretical elegance, one would on the grounds of ease of understanding and ease of computer implementation.

When the set of possible natural language expressions is too large to make the Best Fit method computationally attractive, then the method of Successive Approximation may be used [Clements, 1977]. In this method, one "brackets" the given fuzzy set by the two closest primary terms—one from the "low" end of the rating scale and one from the "high" end. The various hedges are then applied to these bracket endpoints and, if the resulting expression is "closer" to the fuzzy set being approximated, then the bracket is replaced by the hedged term. When these endpoints are as close as possible (in the set of natural language hedged expressions in the rating language), then the distance from the fuzzy set being approximated to three other fuzzy sets is calculated. These three sets are the lower bracket endpoint (possibly a hedged primary, possibly just a primary), the higher bracket endpoint, and the ranged phrase constructed from the lower bracket endpoint and the higher bracket endpoint. The natural language expression corresponding to the closest of these is considered to be the closest natural language expression to the given fuzzy set. The method of Successive Approximation has the advantage of "culling out" a large number of the possible natural language expressions without requiring extensive computations. It is, therefore, more computationally efficient than the Best Fit method. This advantage is especially pronounced if the number of primary terms is greater than three.

The remaining method of finding a natural language expression to represent a given fuzzy set is the method of Piecewise Decomposition. This method, described in Eshragh and Mamdani, [1979], divides the base variable (the numerical variable upon which the linguistic variable is defined) into intervals in such a way that the particular fuzzy set we are interested in approximating, when restricted to each interval, corresponds to a portion of a fuzzy set easily described by one of our natural language expressions. The natural language expressions corresponding to each interval are then combined with one of the standard logical connectives, 'and' or 'or'. While one might expect such a scheme to result in extremely long and non-intuitive expressions, this is not the case with the Eshragh and Mamdani system. They have found techniques to reduce expressions to their "lowest linguistic terms," e.g., reducing 'NOT ABOVE X AND NOT BELOW X' to 'X', as well as methods for efficiently determining the interval breakpoints for the decomposition of the input fuzzy set. One interesting feature of this scheme is that it does not require the input to be a normalized, convex fuzzy set. The Piecewise Decomposition method does, however, require some complicated processing and is non-trivial to implement on a computer.

If the automated risk analysis facility allows a user to provide his own fuzzy meanings for the primary terms or the hedges, it is this problem of mapping from the computed fuzzy set back to a natural language expression that will be complicated the most. Any of the three methods detailed above could be used but with a great deal of generality built into their implementations—generality that must be designed into the implementation from the onset, not retro—fit at a later time.

Chapter 4

PSYCHOLOGICAL CONSIDERATIONS OF FUZZINESS

One might wonder if the considerable trouble we have gone to in order to allow for the input of natural language expressions (as opposed to the input of numerical estimates) is worth the end result? Intuitively (to this author), this effort seems to be the natural result of attempting to provide the most natural and easily learned input method to the computer-naive user. As long as the behind-the-scenes processing of these natural language expressions is compatible with the intuitive meanings given to these expressions by most people, then the effort results in an input method that seems both quite natural and easily used and, therefore, is well worth it. It is comforting to have a number of experimental results which support the compatibility of our fuzzy set meanings for natural language terms with the meanings that are normally given to those terms by most people.

With regard to this estimation of a known imprecise variable either numerically or in natural language terms, one researcher has stated:

> A higher degree of response consistency over trials was found to occur if the subject is allowed to give an imprecise verbal response about a fuzzy (concept) than if he is forced to give a precise "grade-of-membership" answer [Kochen, 1975].

and this conclusion is not restricted to researchers who have been affected by the wide-spread influence of fuzzy set theory. One pre-fuzzy researcher studying the adequacy of everyday language expressions for ratings stated:

> The results of these tests show that such (natural language) terms for describing qualities are very ambiguous; yet for certain purposes, as for example with rating scales, it may be better to use such terms, which everyday people can understand, than to ask judges to attempt the more abstract task of judging by a points (sic) system [Shepard, 1954].

In Nagy and Hoffman [1981] the applicability of natural language input is tested for the specific domain of risk analysis.

Nagy and Hoffman [Nagy and Hoffman, 1981] conducted a preliminary study of the performance differences between subjects using natural language estimates and those using numerical estimates in the task of assessing the security risks of various computer installation configurations. Though this study used few subjects, it indicated that the use of natural language estimates rather than numerical estimates "was associated with an increase in accuracy ranging from 16% to 32% due to elimination of extremely inaccurate estimates." This work demonstrates, albeit only at the level of a preliminary study, the value of using natural language estimates compared to numerical ones in situations like computer security risk analysis where cognitive overload occurs because of either inherent imprecision or overall complexity, especially when the analysis must be carried out by people other than experts.

While the Nagy and Hoffman study dramatically supports the usefulness of the notion of a linguistic variable, it is interesting to note that some researchers feel such results may be applicable to only a portion of the population. Kochen [1975] argues that the general population can be divided into a number of disjoint classes, three of which he calls "estimators," "thresholders," and "reliables." When confronted with a task like stating how strongly they believe that "x is a large number" (for various values of x), "estimators" gauge their strength of belief according to how large they think x is, "thresholders" only according to whether or not x is above an internal threshold, and "reliables" reply either in the extremes (agree strongly or disagree strongly) or not at all. Kochen's work leads him to the conclusion that

> Fuzzy set theory applied to psychology might be interpreted to suggest the general hypothesis that most people are "estimators" rather than "thresholders" or "reliables."

and that

> On the whole, fuzzy set theory does seem appropriate for conceptualizing certain aspects of the behavior of perhaps half the population (the "estimators").

The Nagy and Hoffman study and, to a certain extent, the Kochen work addresses only this natural language input *style*; however, it does not address the method by which these natural language expressions are modeled within a risk analysis utility. With indications that this natural language input style results in such dramatic improvements, the importance of verifying (and possibly improving) the behind-the-scenes modeling of the natural language terms is greatly increased.

The use of fuzzy sets in this behind-the-scenes modeling to directly represent the primitives and to indirectly represent the hedges of natural language expressions is in accordance with the psychological studies of the way people use such expressions [Hersh and Caramazza, 1976]. It has been shown that people naturally form fuzzy sets when categorizing objects, for example, when classifying the vague category of "birdness." Is a robin a bird? And to what extent? What about a penguin?, a bat? ([Heider, 1971], [Macvicar-Whelen, 1978], [McCloskey and Glucksberg, 1978], [Oden, 1977]) By saying that people form fuzzy sets when dealing with such vague concepts, we mean that the way people manipulate these concepts (as evidenced by their responses to various experiments) is very much like the manipulations we have defined for fuzzy sets. This fuzziness is not just the result of averaging the test responses of a number of subjects; it can also be seen in the responses of a single subject [Rubin, 1979].

In addition, a fuzzy set representation for concepts is entirely compatible with both of the currently accepted psychological theories for the inner workings of semantic memory—the memory people have for non-autobiographical information like language, scholastically-acquired information, and knowledge about the interrelationships of concepts in the real world. Both the network model of semantic memory (as typified by the work of Collins and Quillian [1969][1] and Collins and Loftus [1975][2] as well as the feature model of semantic memory of Smith, Shoben, and Rips [1974][3] either had originally or were extended to incorporate fuzzy semantic information processing. In the network model, in

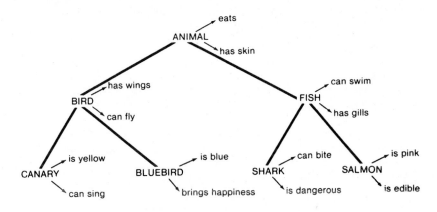

Figure 4.1 Network Representation of Semantic Memory
(After Collins & Quillian, 1969).

[1]Collins, A. M., & Quillian, M. R. Retrieval time from semantic memory, *Journal of Verbal Learning & Verbal Behavior*, vol. 8, (1969), 240—248.
[2]Collins, A.M., & Loftus, E. F. A Spreading-Activation Theory of Semantic Processing, *Psychological Review*, vol. 82, 6, (1975), 407—428.
[3]Smith, E. E., Shoben, E. J., & Rips, L. J. Structure & Process in Semantic Memory: A Featural Model for Semantic Decisions, *Psychological Review*, vol. 81, 3, (1974), 214—241.

which semantic memory is modeled as a hierarchical structure of primitive propositions (the network model representation of a portion of semantic memory is shown in Figure 4.1), one merely has to make these primitive propositions fuzzy, i.e., to associate a degree of truthfulness to them, in order to extend the network model to include fuzzy information processing. Thus, for example, one could associate a degree of truthfulness of 0.8 with the primitive proposition "can fly" associated with the concept of "BIRD." In the feature model, which models concepts in semantic memory as combinations of primitive features, each feature present to various degrees for different concepts, the basic notions of fuzzy information processing were incorporated into the theory from the onset, but this portion of the theory was not often used to explain the experimental data the theory purported to model. Some authors have seen this modification of semantic memory theories as part of the inevitable process of sophistication of a theory in light of additional experimental findings:

> Treating class membership as a discrete all-or-none relation has been very convenient in developing models of semantic memory and semantic information processing. In the beginning stages of model construction, such oversimplifications are typically necessary to keep the whole problem within manageable limits. However, as models mature, convenient oversimplifications usually become neither convenient nor simplifying: the attempt to fit more and more sophisticated phenomena within an overly weak theoretical framework generally results in complex and often grossly contorted descriptions.
>
> In this light, it would appear to be a very healthy sign that many of the important models of semantic memory have now incorporated mechanisms for representing fuzzy semantic information and that inference and retrieval processes have also been proposed, which depend on and capitalize upon the fuzzy information. This is a very important beginning, since higher level semantic processes will build upon the fundamental structures and processes [Oden, 1977].

It is interesting to note that while people comprehend vague concepts *as if* the concepts are internally represented as fuzzy sets, they do not always manipulate these concepts in *exactly* the same ways that we have chosen to manipulate fuzzy sets. While mathematically we have defined the union and the intersection of two fuzzy sets, A and B, in the following manner:

$$A = \{a(x)/x \mid x \in U\}$$
$$B = \{b(x)/x \mid x \in U\}$$

$$A \cup B = \{max(a(x), b(x))/x \mid x \in U\}$$
$$A \cap B = \{min(a(x), b(x))/x \mid x \in U\}$$

and this definition has been shown to be *the only possible* definition naturally extending the notions of union and intersection to the realm of fuzzy sets, Oden has claimed [Oden, 1977] that, experimentally, people logically manipulate vague concepts as if they were fuzzy sets, governed by the following definitions for fuzzy intersection and fuzzy union:

$$A \cap B = \{(a(x) \times b(x))/x \mid x \in U\}$$
$$A \cup B = \{(a(x) + b(x) - a(x) \times b(x))/x \mid x \in U\}$$

While Oden admits that the maximum and minimum rules for forming the union and intersection of fuzzy sets were reasonable explanations of his experimental results, the "multiplying" rules given above "provided a substantially better fit to the data for every (data) matrix and for the great majority of the subjects" [Oden, 1977].

These "multiplying rules" while supported by experimental data, were not derived from an analysis of that data but rather by the consequences of a few subjective decisions. Goguen [1969] postulated two possible intuitively attractive models for fuzzy intersection: the minimum rule that we have explained at length and the multiplying rule:

$$A \cap B = \{(a(x) \times b(x))/x \mid x \in U\}$$

(Note that like the minimum rule, the multiplying rule also reduces to ordinary intersection if the fuzzy sets A and B are ordinary sets, i.e., if they only have degrees of membership of 0 or 1 for all their elements.) The obvious definition for logical negation was also intuitively appealing:

$$A' = \{(1 - a(x)/x \mid x \in U\}$$

If one now assumes DeMorgan's Laws to hold (on the surface a most reasonable assumption, but recall our intuition about what fuzzy sets "ought" to do has led us down strange paths before!), then the "multiplying" rule for fuzzy union can be derived:

$$
\begin{aligned}
A \cup B &= (A' \cap B')' \\
&= \{(1 - \alpha(x))/x \mid x \in U\} \\
&\quad \text{where } \alpha(x) = (1 - a(x)) \times (1 - b(x)) \\
&\quad\quad\quad\quad\quad = 1 - a(x) - b(x) + a(x)b(x) \\
&= \{(a(x) + b(x) - a(x)b(x)) / x \mid x \in U\}
\end{aligned}
$$

So the real difference between these two families of definitions for the operations of fuzzy union and fuzzy intersection is only the definition of fuzzy intersection. While only one of these is mathematically plausible (the minimum rule), there exists excellent philosophical justification for the other, the multiplying rule [Oden, 1979]. Deciding which of these definitions to use is a difficult matter, but one recent examination of this problem has resulted in the following conclusions:

> the choice of (the definition of) an operator is always a matter of context, mainly depending upon the real-world situation which is to be modeled. In other words, all mathematical properties regarding the class of fuzzy set-theoretic operators must be interpreted at an intuitive level [Dubois and Prade, 1980].

Both Hersh and Caramazza [1976] and Macvicar-Whelen [1978] have exhibited experimental data demonstrating that the "traditional" fuzzy modeling of the hedge 'very' is also slightly off. Instead of modeling 'very' as the *CON* operator on the fuzzy set being modified, both these researchers suggest a shift of the fuzzy set. Thus, for example, if the vague concept of 'agile' is modeled by the fuzzy set $A = \{a(x)/x \mid x \in U\}$, then experimental results of the way people use the hedge 'very' suggest that 'very agile' should be modeled by a shift by a constant c, resulting in a fuzzy set

$$\{(a(x) + c)/x \mid x \in U\}$$

rather than the set

$$\{a^2(x)/x \mid x \in U\}$$

as we have suggested earlier when modeling 'very' with the *CON* operator. The differences between these two modelings of 'very' are shown graphically in Figure 4.2.

A totally different argument about the semantics of "very" is offered by Schefe:

> Consider the definition of "very" as a "concentrator" yielding the squares of the fuzzy values operated on. Again there is neither intuitive nor experimental evidence for this definition. ... Attaching a hedge to a concept referring to a continuous scale means creating a new antonym. For example, attaching "very" to the concept "old" creates the new antonym "very old" as opposed to "old." Thus "old" can change its meaning in this (new) context. ...(Another example of this phenomenon of the introduction of "very" changing the meanings of the *other* terms is) if a teacher is asked to classify his students according to "good" and "very good" [Schefe, 1980].

Thus, we see that the available linguistic and psychological literature shows some discrepancy with the mathematical theory of fuzzy sets, both in the abstract manipulation of fuzzy sets (union and intersection) and in the application of these concepts for modeling other abstract notions (hedges).

In the particular case of the hedge 'very' it may be that the situation is just more complex than we first imagined. 'Very' could very well have several modelings dependent on its context.

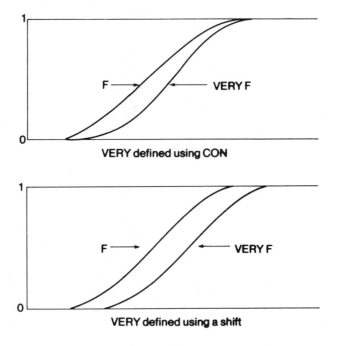

Figure 4.2 Two Meanings for 'VERY'.

Intuitively, it appears that the meaning of *very* in *very large* is qualitatively different from *very* in *very British*. The former implies an extreme of a continuum; the latter implies a greater emphasis on characteristic features [Hersh and Caramazza, 1976].

In the words of the linguist Lakoff, "My feeling at present is that a complete understanding of VERY is very far from our grasp." [Lakoff, 1973].

To be fair, we must also note that two of the most important modeling choices we have made with regard to the manipulation of fuzzy sets *have* been experimentally verified. Both the use of the fuzzy complement to model 'not' as well as the entire notion of modeling hedges as operators on fuzzy sets—operators that can be concatenated using the composition of mathematical functions—have been shown to correlate very well to experimentally derived data reflecting the way people normally use these expressions [Hersh and Caramazza, 1976]. What remains as a "disagreement" between mathematics and psychology is the *exact form* which those operators should take.

Chapter 5

THE FUZZY RISK ANALYZER

The ideas about an automated risk analysis utility presented in this text have been implemented by the Computer Security Research Group at The George Washington University. This utility, called the Fuzzy Risk Analyzer (FRA), is now being evaluated in a research environment to ascertain how closely it achieves the design goals that have been specified in the preceding sections. It is also being used experimentally in some "real world" risk evaluations. An enhanced version of the FRA, entitled IPIRISK, is also being used in some commercial risk analysis evaluations carried out by Information Policy, Inc., a Washington-based consulting firm.

The overall structure of the FRA is shown in Figure 5.1. Basically the FRA consists of three major modules, PARSE, CALC, and LING, which, respectively, translate natural language expressions to discrete fuzzy sets over the universe $\{1, 2, 3, 4, 5, 6, 7, 8, 9\}$, combine these fuzzy sets to calculate the fuzzy set representing the risk of the entire system, and map this resultant fuzzy set back to a natural language expression. The first and third of these operations are essentially as described earlier. The translation to fuzzy sets from the natural language input expressions follows our model for the implementation of both primary terms and hedges with subroutines like VERY, MORL (more or less), FAIRLY, SLIGHTLY, etc., providing the appropriate operations for constructing fuzzy sets to represent natural language expressions like 'MORE OR LESS VERY LOW.' The mapping back to natural language expressions uses the Best Fit method, the method which calculates the Euclidean distance between the computed fuzzy set and the fuzzy sets which represent the various natural language expressions. The user currently does not have the ability to complicate this process of mapping back into natural language terms by providing his own fuzzy meanings for either the primary terms or the hedges.

The second major module in the FRA is concerned with a topic which we have not yet addressed: the computation of the risk for the entire system given the fuzzily estimated risks for the components of the system. There is, of course, no *established* or *standard* way of performing this calculation. To find the mean of a number of natural language risk estimates (forgetting for the moment about the

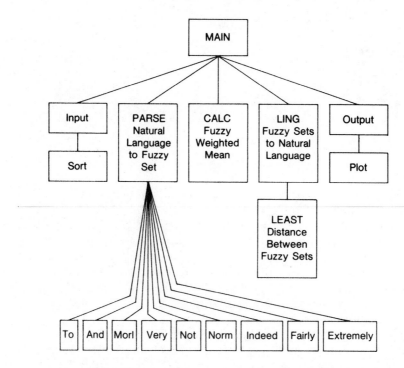

Figure 5.1 Structure of the Fuzzy Risk Analyzer.

complication of weights), one could choose as simple-minded a method as ranking each of the natural language expressions (e.g., VERY LOW = 1, LOW = 2, FAIRLY LOW = 3, ..., HIGH = 33, VERY HIGH = 34) and then just average the ranks in order to average the natural language expressions. Such a scheme would result in such reasonable estimates as

$$\frac{\text{MEDIUM} + \text{MEDIUM}}{2} = \text{MEDIUM}$$

$$\frac{\text{LOW} + \text{MEDIUM} + \text{HIGH}}{3} = \text{MEDIUM}$$

However, this simple scheme fails to model the subtleties and complexities of natural language expressions and is, therefore, little better than a sham—'fooling the novice user,' at its worst. While such a scheme has been used (Note: the reference is intentionally omitted!), no serious proposal will be made here for the adoption of such a trick—it would be a waste of the fuzzy set basis for our natural language expressions.

We wish, therefore, to present a method that will meaningfully combine the fuzzy sets we have so laboriously constructed to represent the natural language estimates. This method, unlike the simple averaging scheme detailed above, will then provide us with a technique for this crucial fuzzy calculation - a technique that has a sound theoretical basis for future research. Before we can address this process in detail we must examine at some length the way risk analysts make use of a tool such as the FRA.

As was stated in the Introduction, an automated risk analysis utility assists a risk analyst in overcoming two problems: overall complexity and inherent imprecision. The key notion here is *"assists."* The FRA assists the user in overcoming inherent imprecision by providing for the input of natural language estimates for imprecise quantities. Hopefully, with some understanding of the way these natural language estimates are used (gained, say, from a thorough and detailed examination of this text!), these natural language estimates will prove to be reliable and believable ratings. The other problem, overall complexity, is partially solved by the use of the FRA itself and partially solved by the methodology that its use forces on the user. The FRA can compute the overall risk for a system composed of many components - but only if the user can provide the appropriate decomposition of the system into its component parts. This methodology itself partially solves the problem of overall complexity and also improves the ultimate rating because "a composite rating based upon an exhaustive detailed decomposition will be less likely to omit significant components" [Clements, 1977]. This methodology is further enhanced (and enforced) by the FRA input forms, one of which is reproduced as Figure 5.2. That input form forces the user to describe his system hierarchically (with a number of levels using multiple input forms). However, something we have not mentioned up to this point, is that the FRA not only allows the user to provide a fuzzy estimate of the probability of failure of a particular component (e.g., the failure of the cypher lock component of the computer security system), but it also allows a fuzzy estimate of the importance of each component to the whole—a fuzzy weight—as well as a fuzzy estimate of the reliability of the fuzzy estimates made by the user. The FRA makes use of all this information in determining the overall risk of the entire system.

Figure 5.3 shows a typical, though rather small, input to the FRA. Let us step through the computations done by the FRA in determining the overall system risk. Because this example is small, we have only to calculate the "fuzzy weighted average" of the three root nodes on the tree in Figure 5.3 in order to compute the total risk. In a larger, more general case, one merely climbs the tree of the system decomposition computing the risk of each interior node from the risk values of its

The George Washington University
Department of Electrical Engineering and Computer Science
Computer Security and Risk Assessment Research Project

RISK INPUT FORM
SYSTEM DESCRIPTION WITH RISK ESTIMATES

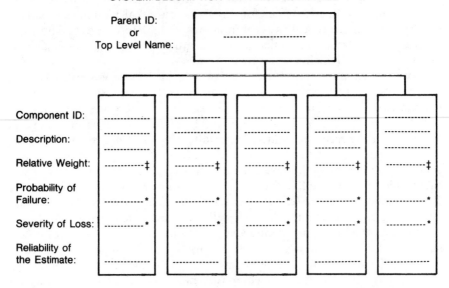

Your task consists of the following four steps:

(1) Assign a hierarchical identifier for each component.
(2) Provide a description of each. You can use up to 20 characters.
(3) Estimate the probability that the component will fail. (Or its weight if not lowest level).
(4) *Estimate the severity of loss of the component. This is, what the loss would be if this component fails.
(5) Estimate the reliability of these two estimates (Blank = high, R = reasonable, B = barely reliable).

H = high, M = medium, L = low, N = not, F = fairly, V = very, 0 = more or less, T = to
----

*To be completed only for lowest level components
‡To be completed only for non-lowest level components

Figure 5.2 FRA Input Form.

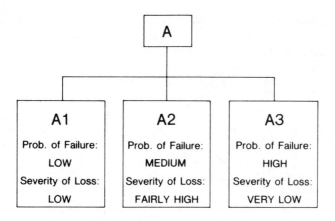

Figure 5.3 FRA Example.

descendants, until one arrives at the root node. In our abbreviated example, the initial step and this final step happen to be identical.

The possibility of loss, the severity of loss, and the reliability estimate for each descendant of a given node are all taken into account in order to calculate the total risk for the node, although in this small example the reliabiity estimates are ignored. The calculation is the fuzzy weighted mean, a generalization of the normal weighted mean defined over, for example, the integers. Recall that if $\{R_i\}$ is a sequence of integers, and $\{W_i\}$ a sequence of integer weights, then the weighted mean of the R_i's is defined as:

$$\overline{W} = \frac{\displaystyle\sum_{i=1}^{n} W_i \times R_i}{\displaystyle\sum_{i=1}^{n} W_i}$$

We will extend this definition to provide a similar computation where both the entities being weighted and their weights are fuzzy quantities. To do this we must extend the arithmetic operations used in the computation of the mean: addition, multiplication, and division, from operators defined on the reals to operators defined for fuzzy sets. This will be done using Zadeh's extension principle, a general method for extending functions over the integers to functions over fuzzy subsets based over the integers. (An alternative way of defining fuzzy addition is given in Dubois and Prade, [1979B].) Since the actual details of the use of the extension principle are somewhat complex, they are presented in Appendix II.

The results from this use of the extension principle are the following definitions (over the universe $\{1, 2, 3, 4, 5, 6, 7, 8, 9\}$) for fuzzy addition, fuzzy multiplication, and fuzzy division: Let

$$A = \{a(i)/i \mid 1 \leq i \leq 9\}$$

$$B = \{b(j)/j \mid 1 \leq j \leq 9\}$$

then

$$A + B = \{min(a(i), b(j))/[i + j] \mid 1 \leq i, j \leq 9\}$$

$$A * B = \{min(a(i), b(j))/[i * j] \mid 1 \leq i, j \leq 9\}$$

$$A \mid B = \{min(a(i), b(j))/[i \mid j] \mid 1 \leq i, j \leq 9\}$$

What this definition means computationally is that to compute the degree of membership of, say, 8 in $A + B$, we have to examine all of the possible ways that two integers (taken from the set $\{1, 2, 3, 4, 5, 6, 7, 8, 9\}$) can sum to 8 and examine the degrees of membership of these pairs. Thus, if the degree of membership of 8 in $A + B$ was x, then x would be computed as follows:

$$x = max\{min(a(1), b(7)), min(a(2), b(6)), min(a(3), b(5)), min(a(4), b(4)),$$
$$min(a(5), b(3)), min(a(6), b(2)), min(a(7), b(1))\}.$$

Each of the minimum operations computes one of the degrees of membrship of 8 in the set $A + B$. We then take the greatest such degree of membership to be *the* degree of membership of 8. The maximum is used because

$$\{x, y, y, z\} = \{x, y, z\} \quad \text{(in ordinary set theory)}$$

and

$$\{.1/x, .2/y, .4/y, .9/z\} = \{.1/x, .4/y, .9/z\} \quad \text{(in fuzzy set theory)}$$

Notice that $A + B$ is a fuzzy subset over the set of integers from 1 to 18, $A * B$ is a fuzzy subset over the set of integers from 1 to 81, and $A \mid B$ is a mess. In theory, $A \mid B$ should be a fuzzy subset over the set of *reals* from 1 to 9—in most implementations, however, this must be approximated. In Clements, [1977] this set over the reals is reduced to one over the integers by *deleting* any element not over an integer base. Currently in the FRA, this reduction from a fuzzy set over the reals to one over the integers is done by assigning the following degree of membership to the integer k:

$$\underset{(i/j) \,\epsilon\, [k,\, k\,+\,1)}{\text{MAX}} \quad \{min(a(i),\, b(j))\}$$

Using the definition given above for fuzzy addition, fuzzy multiplication, and fuzzy division (the Clements method), we can then define the fuzzy weighted mean: Let $\{R_i\}$ and $\{W_i\}$ be a sequence of fuzzy sets. Then the fuzzy mean of the R_i's using the W_i's as weights is

$$\overline{W} = \frac{\sum_{i=1}^{n} W_i \times R_i}{\sum_{i=1}^{n} W_i}$$

where *all* the fuzzy arithmetic operations are represented by symbols for their normal arithmetic counterparts. (The reader is warned that this is something almost all researchers in fuzzy set theory do—supposedly it aids in intuition, but many times it is a terrible stumbling block to the fuzzy novice. For those familiar with terminology used with the new programming language Ada, we have just *overloaded* the operators $+$, $*$, and $/$.)

For reasons which may at this point be clear to the reader (or will very shortly become clear), it is not feasible to perform the FRA calculations by hand for our example in Figure 5.3 if the universe over which the fuzzy sets are defined is the set $\{1, 2, 3, 4, 5, 6, 7, 8, 9\}$. We will, therefore, restrict the universe to $\{1, 2, 3, 4\}$ and make the following definitions of the fuzzy meanings for five natural language expressions:

Expression	Fuzzy Meaning
VERY LOW	$\{1.0/1, \ .2/2, \ 0/3, \ 0/4\}$
LOW	$\{1.0/1, \ .6/2, \ .1/3, \ 0/4\}$
MEDIUM	$\{ .2/1, \ 1.0/2, \ 1.0/3, \ .2/4\}$
FAIRLY HIGH	$\{ 0/1, \ .2/2, \ .9/3, \ .7/4\}$
HIGH	$\{ 0/1, \ .1/2, \ .6/3, \ 1.0/4\}$

(Recall that we are not required to justify these definitions. They are *a priori* decisions of the system designer.)

The FRA definition of the total risk for the system in Figure 5.3 (or equivalently in our small example, the risk associated with the node 'A') is:

$$\frac{(\text{LOW} * \text{LOW}) + (\text{MEDIUM} * \text{FAIRLY HIGH}) + (\text{HIGH} * \text{VERY LOW})}{\text{LOW} + \text{FAIRLY HIGH} + \text{VERY LOW}}$$

where the probabilities of failure are the W_i's and the severities of loss are the R_i's and where $+$, $*$ and / have their overloaded fuzzy meanings. Because we are using these overloaded meanings, this calculation takes into account all of the "fuzziness" inherent in our representation of these natural language expressions. What we have done is to naturally extend (using the extension principle) the weighted mean defined for the integers to the fuzzy weighted mean of fuzzy values in a systematic and theoretically-sound manner.

While this definition of the fuzzy weighted mean was obtained as a reasonable extension from the definition of the normal weighted mean calculation, the issues are not so clear as might seem at first glance. It often happens that each individual researcher has his own intuitive notions about about how concepts such as means should behave, and it is not always possible to preserve all such intuitions when extending definitions to the realm of fuzzy sets. The best we can reasonably hope for is to preserve most of them. In this regard, it would be most unfortunate if our definition of the fuzzy weighted mean did not preserve identities like:

$$\frac{\text{LOW} + \text{LOW}}{2} = \text{LOW}$$

Fortunately, it does. We can demonstrate this by means of a small example. Let

$W_1 = \{1.0/1\},$ *(the weight 1)*
$R_1 = \{1.0/1, 0.6/2, 0.1/3, 0.0/4\},$ *(one possible definition for the fuzzy set LOW)*
$W_2 = \{1.0/1\},$ and
$R_2 = \{1.0/1, 0.6/2, 0.1/3, 0.0/4\}.$

Then

$$\overline{W} = \frac{\sum\limits_{i=1}^{2} W_i \times R_i}{\sum\limits_{i=1}^{2} W_i} = \frac{(W_1 \times R_1) + (W_2 \times R_2)}{W_i + W_2}$$

We calculate

$$W_1 + W_2 = \{\min(1.0, 1.0)/[1 + 1]\} = \{1.0/2\} = \{0/1, 1.0/2\},$$

$W_1 \times R_1 = W_2 \times R_2 =$
   $\{\min(1.0, \ 1.0)/[1 \ \times \ 1], \ \min(1.0, \ 0.6)/[1 \ \times \ 2], \ \min(1.0, \ 0.1)/[1 \ \times \ 3],$
      $\min(1.0, \ 0)/[1 \times 4]\}$
   $= \{1.0/1, 0.6/2, 0.1/3, 0/4\}$
   $= R_1 = R_2,$

$(W_1 \times R_1) + (W_2 \times R_2) =$
   $\{1.0/1, 0.6/2, 0.1/3, 0/4\} + \{1.0/1, 0.6/2, 0.1/3, 0/4\} =$

   $\{\min(1.0,1.0)/[1 + 1],$
   $\min(1.0, 0.6)/[1 + 2], \min(0.6, 1.0)/[2 + 1],$
   $\min(1.0, 0.1)/[1 + 3], \min(0.6, 0.6)/[2 + 2], \min(0.1, 1.0)/[3 + 1],$
   $\min(1.0, 0.0)/[1 + 4], \min(0.6, 0.1)/[2 + 3], \min(0.1, 0.6)/[3 + 2], \min(0.0,$
      $1.0)/[4 + 1]$
   $\min(0.6, 0.0)/[2 + 4], \min(0.1, 0.1)/[3 + 3], \min(0.0, 0.6)/[4 + 2],$
   $\min(0.1, 0.0)/[3 + 4], \min(0.0, 0.1)/[4 + 3],$
   $\min(0.0, 0.0)/[4 + 4]\}$
   $= \{1.0/2, 0.6/3, 0.6/4, 0.1/5, 0.1/6, 0/7, 0/8\}$

Thus,

$$\frac{(W_1 \times R_1) + (W_2 \times R_2)}{W_1 + W_2} = \frac{\{1.0/2, 0.6/3, 0.6/4, 0.1/5, 0.1/6, 0.0/7, 0.0/8\}}{\{0.0/1, 1.0/2\}}$$

$$= \{a/1, b/2, c/3, d/4\}$$

where

   $a = \max(1.0, 1.0)$ *(the [2 ÷ 2] component)*
   $b = \max(\min(1.0, 0.0), \min(0.6, 1.0))$ *(the [2 ÷ 1] and [4 ÷ 2] components)*
   $c = \max(\min(0.6, 0.0), \min(0.1, 1.0))$ *(the [3 ÷ 1] and [6 ÷ 2] components),*
      and
   $d = \max(\min(0.6, 0.0), \min(0.0, 1.0))$ *(the [4 ÷ 1] and [8 ÷ 2] components).*

Thus,

$$\overline{W} = R_1 = R_2$$

or equivalently,

$$\frac{\text{LOW} + \text{LOW}}{2} = \text{LOW}$$

With our confidence in our definition of the fuzzy weighted mean thus reinforced, let us carry out the computation for the system in Figure 5.3. First we must compute the partial sum LOW + FAIRLY HIGH. Since

$$\text{LOW} = \{1.0/1, .6/2, .1/3, 0/4\}$$

and

$$\text{FAIRLY HIGH} = \{0/1, .2/2, .9/3, .7/4\}$$

then

LOW + FAIRLY HIGH =

$\{min(1.0, 0)/[1 + 1],$
$min(1.0, .2)/[1 + 2], min(.6, 0)/[2 + 1],$
$min(1.0, .9)/[1 + 3], min(.6, .2)/[2 + 2], min(.1, 0)/[3 + 1],$
$min(1.0, .7)/[1 + 4], min(.6, .9)/[2 + 3], min(.1, .2)/[3 + 2], min(0.0)/[4, 1],$
$min(.6, .7)/[2 + 4], min(.1, .9)/[3 + 3], min(0, .2)/[4 + 2],$
$min(.1, .7)/[3 + 4], min(0, .9)/[4 + 3],$
$min(0, .7)/[4 + 4]\}$
  $= \{ 0/2, .2/3, 0/3, .9/4, .2/4, 0/4, .7/5, .6/5, .1/5, 0/5, .6/6, .1/6, 0/6,$
    $.1/7, 0/7, 0/8\}$
  $= \{0/1, 0/2, .2/3, .9/4, .7/5, .6/6, .1/7, 0/8\}$

and after normalization

$$= \{0/1, 0/2, .22/3, 1.0/4, .77/5, .66/6, .11/7, 0/8\}.$$

and we see that this is a convex fuzzy set, so the convexity operation does not modify it. (Note: It should be clear why the reduction in the size of the universe was made for the purposes of this example. If it is not, please repeat the above computation for fuzzy sets over the universe of $\{1, 2, 3, 4, 5, 6, 7, 8, 9\}$!)

Making a similar computation we obtain:

LOW + FAIRLY HIGH + VERY LOW =
$\{0/1, 0/2, 0/3, .22/4, 1.0/5, .77/6, .66/7, .22/8, .11/9, 0/10, 0/11, 0/12\}$

This fuzzy set will be the denominator in the fuzzy weighted mean calculation to determine the risk of the entire system. Note that even though the universe of the primitive terms is {1, 2, 3, 4}, the sum of *three* such terms will be a fuzzy set over {1, 2, 3, 4, 5, 6, 7, 8, 9, 10, 11, 12}. Realizing that this is as it should be, it becomes very clear why so many implementations of fuzzy set applications are done in APL, a language that allows very flexible vector manipulations and in particular allows vectors to "grow" in length.

Now let us compute the product MEDIUM * FAIRLY HIGH. Recall that

$$\text{MEDIUM} = \{.2/1,\ 1.0/2,\ 1.0/3,\ .2/4\}$$

and

$$\text{FAIRLY HIGH} = \{0/1,\ .2/2,\ .9/3,\ .7/4\}.$$

Then, according to our earlier definition of the fuzzy product:

MEDIUM * FAIRLY HIGH =

$\{min(\ .2, 0)/[1*1],$
$min(\ .2,.2)/[1*2],\ min(1.0, 0)/[2*1],$
$min(\ .2,.9)/[1*3],\ min(1.0, 0)/[3*1],$
$min(\ .2,.7)/[1*4],\ min(1.0,.2)/[2*2],\ min(.2,0)/[4*1],$
$min(1.0,.9)/[2*3],\ min(1.0,.2)/[3*2],$
$min(1.0,.7)/[2*4],\ min(\ .2,.2)/[4*2],$
$min(1.0,.9)/[3*3],$
$min(1.0,.7)/[3*4],\ min(\ .2,.9)/[4*3],$
$min(\ .2,.7)/[4*4]\}$

$= \{0/1,\ .2/2,\ 0/2,\ .2/3,\ 0/3,\ .2/4,\ .2/4,\ 0/4,$
$\qquad .9/6,\ .2/6,\ .7/8,\ .2/8,\ .9/9,\ .7/12,\ .2/12,\ .2/16\}$

$= \{0/1,\ .2/2,\ .2/3,\ .2/4,\ .9/6,\ .7/8,\ .9/9,\ .7/12,\ .2/16\}$

Normalizing, we obtain

$= \{0/1,\ .22/2,\ .22/3,\ .22/4,\ 0/5,\ 1.0/6,\ 0/7,\ .77/8,$
$\qquad 1.0/9,\ 0/10,\ 0/11,\ .77/12,\ 0/13,\ 0/14,\ 0/15,\ .22/16\}$

Unfortunately, this is not a convex set, so we adjust the values to maintain convexity. Thus,

MEDIUM * FAIRLY HIGH =
{0/1, .22/2, .22/3, .22/4, .61/5, 1.0/6, 1.0/7, 1.0/8,
1.0/9 .93/10, .85/11, .77/12, .63/13, .50/14, .36/15, .22/16}

Similarly, we can compute, after normalization and convexity modifications:

LOW * LOW =
{1.0/1, .6/2, .6/3, .6/4, .35/5, .1/6, .1/7, .1/8,
.1/9, 0/10, 0/11, 0/12, 0/13, 0/14, 0/15, 0/16}

HIGH * VERY LOW =
{0/1, .1/2, .6/3, 1.0/4, .6/5, .2/6,, .2/7, .2/8,
0/9, 0/10, 0/11, 0/12, 0/13, 0/14, 0/15, 0/16}

Continuing in the computation of the fuzzy weighted mean for the example of Figure 5.3, we calculate:

(LOW * LOW) + (MEDIUM * FAIRLY HIGH) =
{0/1, 0/2, .22/3, .22/4, .22/5, .61/6, 1.0/7, 1.0/8, 1.0/9, 1.0/10, .93/11,
.85/12, .77/13, .64/14, .6/15, .6/16, .6/17, .5/18 .1/25, 0/26, 0/27, 0/28,
0/29, 0/30, 0/31, 0/32}

and

[(LOW * LOW) + (MEDIUM * FAIRLY HIGH)]
     + (HIGH * VERY LOW) =
{0/1, 0/2, 0/3, 0/4, .1/5, .22/6, .22/7, .22/8, .6/9, .61/10, 1.0/11, 1.0/12,
1.0/13, 1.0/14, .93/15, .85/16, .77/17, .64/18, .6/19, .6/20, .6/21, .6/22,
.5/23, .36/24, .35/25, .22/26, .2/27, .2/28, .2/29, .1/30, 1/31, .1/32, .1/33,
0/34, 0/35, 0/36, 0/37, 0/38, 0/39, 0/40, 0/41, 0/42, 0/43, 0/44, 0/45,
0/46, 0/47, 0/48}

The fuzzy division of (LOW * LOW) + (MEDIUM * FAIRLY HIGH) + (HIGH * VERY LOW) by (LOW + FAIRLY HIGH + VERY LOW) can now be done. The method of Clements [Clements, 1977] will be used to map the result of this fuzzy division back into the set of fuzzy subsets of {1, 2, 3, 4}. Recall that the definition of fuzzy division is

$$A \mid B = \{min(a(i), b(j))/[i \mid j] \mid 1 \le i, j \le 9\},$$

and also that the Clements method for obtaining a quotient fuzzy subset of $\{1, 2, 3, 4\}$ (as opposed to a fuzzy subset of the real interval $[1, 4]$) is to ignore any elements of $A \ / \ B$ that are not integers. In addition, Clements also ignored any integer outside the universe of his primary terms when mapping this quotient set back to natural language expressions. We see then that the use of the Clements method implies that only i, j pairs whose quotients are *integers* in the set $\{1, 2, 3, 4\}$ need be computed. In detail then, the computation for the degree of membership of the element 3 in the final fuzzy quotient is as follows: Let $\{a/1, b/2, c/3, d/4\}$ be the fuzzy quotient resulting from the fuzzy division of (LOW $*$ LOW) $+$ (MEDIUM $*$ FAIRLY HIGH) $+$ (HIGH $*$ VERY LOW) $= \{x(i) \mid 1 \le i \le 48\}$, by (LOW $+$ FAIRLY HIGH $+$ VERY LOW) $= \{y(j) \mid 1 \le j \le 9\}$. Then

$$c = max[\ min(x(3), y(1)), min(x(6), y(2)),$$
$$min(x(9), y(3)), min(x(12), y(4)),$$
$$min(x(15), y(5)), min(x(18), y(6)),$$
$$min(x(21), y(7)), min(x(24), y(8)),$$
$$min(x(27), y(9)), min(x(30), y(10)),$$
$$min(x(33), y(11)), min(x(36), y(12))]$$

$$= max[\ min(0,\ 0),\ min(.22, 0),$$
$$min(.6, 0), min(1.0, .22),$$
$$min(.93, 1.0), min(.64, .77),$$
$$min(.6, .66), min(.36, .22),$$
$$min(.2, .11), min(.1, 0),$$
$$min(.1, 0), min(0, 0)]$$

$$= max[0, 0, 0, .22, .93, .64, .6, .22, .11, 0, 0, 0]$$

$$= .93$$

Similar calculations yield a fuzzy quotient of

$$\{.22/1, .77/2, .93/3, .36/4\}$$

After normalization this becomes

$$\{.23/1, .82/2, 1.0/3, .38/4\}$$

Using the Best Fit method, we map this result back to the set of natural language expressions in our small example, {VERY LOW, LOW, MEDIUM, FAIRLY HIGH, HIGH}. Let X be the result of the above fuzzy weighted mean operation. Then the distance from X to LOW can easily be calculated:

$$d(X, \text{LOW}) = \left[\sum_{i=1}^{4} (x(i) - low(i))^2 \right]^{1/2}$$

$$= [(.23 - 1.0)^2 + (.82 - .6)^2 + (1.0 - .1)^2 + (.38 - 0)^2]^{1/2}$$

$$= 1.263$$

Similarly, we can compute

$$d(X, \text{VERY LOW}) = 1.456$$
$$d(X, \text{MEDIUM}) = 0.2184$$
$$d(X, \text{FAIRLY HIGH}) = 0.7414$$
$$d(X, \text{HIGH}) = 1.056$$

Thus, we would report back to the user that the overall risk of the system presented in Figure 5.3 is MEDIUM, because of the five natural language expressions to choose from, MEDIUM is the "closest" (in the sense of Euclidean distance) to the fuzzy set resulting from the fuzzy weighted mean calculation.

Up to this point we have provided the reader with an understanding of how the *internals* of the FRA work: hedges, ranges, fuzzy weighted means, etc. We have not, however, provided any information as to how the *externals* of the FRA utility appear to the user, or how an individual analyst uses the utility to compute the risk associated with a reasonably sized example. While the underlying concepts of fuzzy risk analysis may provide the risk analyst with a powerful mechanism for what is now often called *approximate reasoning*, if the actual mechanisms employed by the user to make use of the FRA are clumsy and/or error prone, the FRA utility will not be useful. A good man-machine dialogue is, thus, critically important in the actual operation of the FRA in order to bring the power of fuzzy reasoning to bear on real problems.

The current user interface for the FRA[1] is constrained by the most commonplace hardware currently used in man-machine interaction: a relatively dumb alphanumeric CRT terminal connected by a relatively low-speed communication line to a mainframe computer. On such an alphanumeric device, it is impossible to actually draw, in an acceptable manner, a tree like that shown in Figure 5.7. To overcome this difficulty, the current user interface approaches the FRA tree through the additional concepts of *levels* and of the current level in the tree. The head node is on level one, its descendants are on level two, their descendants are

---

[1] The vast majority of the credit for this user interface design *and* implementation belongs to Keith Bostic, a member of the George Washington University Computer Security Research Group. The author is indebted to him for the opportunity to experiment with the results of his work and for his permission to document them here.

on level three, etc. Any *one* level of the FRA tree is usually sufficiently simple to be easily represented on an alphanumeric device and, given a sufficiently loose intrepretation of the word "drawn," a single level can even be drawn on such a device. At any one time, the user is positioned at one and only one level of the tree. To select a particular node for any of the possible user actions, (e.g., for deletion, a change in one of its natural language values, or to add a descendant), the user must be positioned at the level of that node. Prior to issuing the desired command, the user must, therefore, either ascend or descend from the current level in the tree to the level of that particular node.

The screen format used by the FRA on the alphanumeric CRT is shown in Figure 5.4. The Current Level Listing Area lists the names of the nodes in the current level. The Command Listing Area lists most of the commands currently available to the user. The Feedback Area is used to display special instructions and error messages and the Interaction Area is an independently scrolling area into which the commands that the user has typed and other routine system confirmations are listed by the system. The FRA user, however, does not see these areas labelled as such. A typical screen image is shown in Figure 5.5 with each of these areas filled in with the types of contents one would see in the middle of a session of using the FRA. The Current Level Listing Area, the Feedback Area and the Interaction Area have dynamic contents. Note that the Feedback

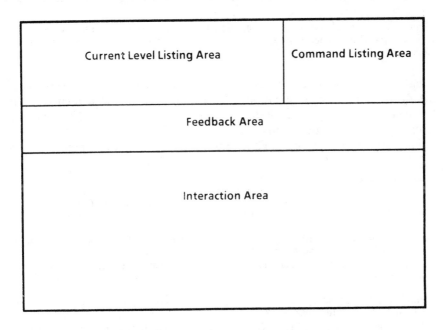

Figure 5.4 The four screen areas of the FRA display.

```
1. Badges                            $      down      print
2. Cipher lock                       !      end       save
3. 24-hr guard                       ?      estimate  set
                                     add    help      show
                                     analyze name     status
                                     delete new      up

---------------------------------------------------------------------

Message:  Node named 24-hr guard added to tree.


---------------------------------------------------------------------


   down


       Which node do you want to descend from?
       Please input a number between 1 and 3.


   1
```

Figure 5.5 A typical screen during the use of the FRA. As is now almost a *de facto* standard for alphanumeric CRTs, the screen displays exactly 24 lines of 80 characters each.

Area which presents special warnings and messages to the user is in the center of the display, the area most visible to the typical user. The contents of the Command Area, unlike that of the other areas, is static.[2] Figure 5.6 details the semantics of each of the commands.

To give the reader an appreciation for the "flavor" of this FRA interface, let us

---

[2]Note that in the absence of any clear structure to the command set, the commands are listed on the screen in alphabetic order, in accordance with "established" ergonomic design principles. For a detailed enumeration of these and other guidelines for the arrangement of alphanumeric displays, see the following references:

Engel, Stephen E., and Richard E. Granda, Guidelines for Man/Display Interfaces, Technical Report TR 00.2720, IBM Poughkeepsie Laboratory, 19 December 1975.

Hansen, Wilfred J., User Engineering Principles for Interactive Systems, *AFIPS Conference Proceedings of the 1971 Fall Joint Computer Conference,* vol. 39, AFIPS Press, Montvale, NJ, 1971, 523-532.

Robertson, P.J., A Guide to Using Color on Alphanumeric Displays, Technical Report, IBM U.K. Laboratories Limited, June 1980.

Shneiderman, Ben, Human Factors Experiments in Designing Interactive Systems, *Computer,* December 1979, 9-19.

Command	Meaning
$	Abort
!	Return (temporarily) to the operating system. Upon issuance of the standard operating system command (e.g., cntl-C), the user is returned to the FRA in the current state.
?	List current available commands and update the screen. (For use in those few screen displays that do not continually list the commands.)
add	Add a new node to the end of the list of nodes at the current level.
analyze	Compute the total risk associated with the entire tree using the fuzzy algorithms explained earlier.
delete	Delete a node at the current level and re-number the remaining nodes.
down	Descend to the next lower level.
end	Terminate the FRA session gracefully.
estimate	Add natural language estimates for the weight, plausibility of failure/loss, reliability of estimates, and severity of failure/loss for a given node.
help	Provide additional help data.
name	Rename a given node.
new	Delete existing tree and start anew.
print	Provide a listing of the current tree, in either indented tree notation or in a semi-graphical notation.
save	Save the current tree in a specified file.
set	Change the values of various parameters, e.g., expert *vs* novice mode.
show	Show the current values of all the parameters.
status	Provide a listing of the path from the lead node to the current level as well as listings of the estimates at the current level.
up	Ascend the tree to the next higher level.

Figure 5.6 FRA Command Semantics.

examine the interaction sequence a user would experience in analyzing the risk of the system presented in Figure 5.7. Figures 5.8 through 5.24 will detail the various screen images seen by the user in the analysis of this system. (For ease of reading, the user entries/responses in the Interaction Area of all these figures will be presented in bold face. This is not in reality how the screen would appear to a user. Most alphanumeric CRTs cannot display easily discerned boldface characters.)

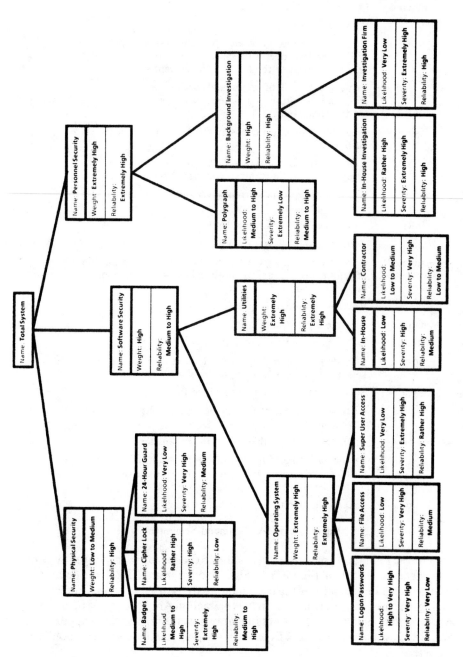

Figure 5.7 Sample System Decomposition for FRA input.

```
 1.                                              $       down      print
                                                 !       end       save
                                                 ?       estimate  set
                                                 add     help      show
                                                 analyze name      status
                                                 delete  new       up
----------------------------------------------------------------------------



----------------------------------------------------------------------------
  Please provide a name for the head node:

Total System



```

Figure 5.8 Initial FRA Screen. Since the FRA input is a hierarchical description of the system to be analyzed, there must be a single head node for the tree that represents this hierarchy. The first action of the FRA is to request a name for this node. Figure 5.9 shows the results of this input in the Current Level Listing Area.

(Note that in this figure and in all following figures depicting the current FRA user interface, user responses are shown in bold face.)

```
 1. Total System                                    $         down       print
                                                    !         end        save
                                                    ?         estimate   set
                                                    add       help       show
                                                    analyze   name       status
                                                    delete    new        up
------------------------------------------------------------------------------



------------------------------------------------------------------------------
   Please enter next command:

down

   To descend the tree you must create a new node.
   Name for this node?

Physical Security



```

Figure 5.9 Descending the tree. The user must execute the **down** command to
descend to a lower level of the tree, in order to add, modify, or delete nodes at that
level. Since the tree currently contains only the head node (and, thus, no nodes at the
level being descended to), the system automatically prompts for a node name for
this level. Figure 5.10 shows the node name the user responded with ("Physical
Security") in the Current Level Listing Area.

```
  1. Physical Security                          $         down        print
                                                !         end         save
                                                ?         estimate    set
                                                add       help        show
                                                analyze   name        status
                                                delete    new         up
------------------------------------------------------------------------------
Message:  Node Physical Security added to tree.


------------------------------------------------------------------------------
    Please enter next command:

add

    Name for this node?

Software Security
```

Figure 5.10 (Part 1). Adding new nodes to the current level. Using the **add**
command new nodes can be added to the current level. Note that the order of this
addition is important. As can be seen in the next figure (Figure 5.11) "Software
Security" becomes the second node on this level and "Personnel Security" becomes
the third. Note, too, that "Total System" is no longer listed in the Current Level
Listing Area since the "Total System" node is not at the current level.

```
1. Physical Security                              $        down      print
2. Software Security                              !        end       save
                                                  ?        estimate  set
                                                  add      help      show
                                                  analyze  name      status
                                                  delete   new       up
-------------------------------------------------------------------------
Message:  Node Software Security added to tree.


-------------------------------------------------------------------------
Please enter next command:

add

   Name for this node?

Personnel Security
```

Figure 5.10 (Part 2) Adding new nodes to the current level. Note that at the completion of each command the Interaction Area is cleared.

```
  1. Physical Security                    $        down      print
  2. Software Security                     !        end       save
  3. Personnel Security                    ?        estimate  set
                                           add      help      show
                                           analyze  name      status
                                           delete   new       up
-----------------------------------------------------------------------
Message:  Node Personnel Security added to tree.


-----------------------------------------------------------------------
   Please enter next command:

down

   Which node do you wish to descend from?
   Please enter a number between 1 and 3.

3

   To descend the tree you must create a new node.
   Name for this node:

Polygraph
```

Figure 5.11 Descending the tree. When descending from a level with more than one node, the system requires that the user specify from which node to descend. *The user thus constructs the FRA tree by his movements between the various levels and the commands he issues between those movements.*

(Contrast this instance of the use of the **down** command with that of Figure 5.9. Since in the situation of Figure 5.9, there was only one node at the current level, the prompting for a node number to descend from did not take place.)

```
1. Polygraph                                    $        down       print
                                                !         end        save
                                                ?      estimate      set
                                              add        help       show
                                          analyze        name       status
                                           delete         new        up
-------------------------------------------------------------------------------
Message:   Node Polygraph added to tree.


-------------------------------------------------------------------------------
   Please enter next command:

estimate

   Enter fuzzy likelyhood of the failure of this node:  Somewhat Low
      "Somewhat Low" is not an acceptable fuzzy expression.
      For a listing of acceptable fuzzy expressions, type "help",
      otherwise, enter new fuzzy estimate:  Low to Medium
   Enter fuzzy confidence of your prediction:  Very Low
   Enter fuzzy severity of the failure of this node:  High
```

Figure 5.12 Adding the natural language estimates for a node. Using the **estimate** command, the user enters the natural language values for the relative weight, plausibility of failure/loss, reliability of the estimates, and severity of the failure/loss. Note that not all of these will be used. Relative weight is used only for non-terminal nodes; plausibility of failure/loss and severity of failure/loss are used only for terminal nodes. In this user interface to the FRA, the user provides only those estimates that apply to the given node. In this particular example, the "Polygraph" node is not given a relative weight estimate since it is a terminal node. If at a later time new nodes are added beneath the "Polygraph" node, a relative weight estimate must then be given for the "Polygraph" node. The other estimates (plausibility and severity) of the "Polygraph" node that are not used (since it is now a non-terminal node) are then just considered to be (temporarily) unnecessary estimates. In the subsequent calculation of the fuzzy weighted mean of the tree, the FRA ignores such unnecessary estimates. Should the "Polygraph" node later become a terminal node (following the deletion of its descendants), these unnecessary estimates would revert to necessary ones and *would not have to be re-entered by the user.*

```
1. Polygraph                              $        down      print
                                          !        end       save
                                          ?        estimate  set
                                          add      help      show
                                          analyze  name      status
                                          delete   new       up
-----------------------------------------------------------------------

-----------------------------------------------------------------------
   Please enter next command:

status
```

Figure 5.13 Requesting a print of the position of the current level. The use of levels to construct the tree has the disadvantage that the user can become "lost". The **status** command lists the path from the head node to the current level and the fuzzy estimates for all nodes at that level. The resulting display is shown in Figure 5.14.

```
1. Polygraph                                      $          down       print
                                                  !          end        save
                                                  ?          estimate   set
                                                  add        help       show
                                                  analyze    name       status
                                                  delete     new        up
------------------------------------------------------------------------------


------------------------------------------------------------------------------
    Name                 Weight        Confidence      Likelihood      Severity

Total System
  Personnel Security
                           --      Currently at this level
     Polygraph            High        Very Low         L to M          High



Please push return to continue:
```

Figure 5.14 The result of the **status** command.

```
1. Polygraph                                      $          down       print
                                                  !          end        save
                                                  ?          estimate   set
                                                  add        help       show
                                                  analyze    name       show
                                                  delete     new        up
------------------------------------------------------------------------------


------------------------------------------------------------------------------
   Please enter next command:

add

   Name for this node:

Background Investigation
```

Figure 5.15 Adding new nodes to the current level.

```
  1. Polygrapn                                          $        down       print
  2. Background Investigation                           !        end        save
                                                        ?        estimate   set
                                                        add      help       show
                                                        analyze  name       status
                                                        delete   new        up
- - - - - - - - - - - - - - - - - - - - - - - - - - - - - - - - - - - - - - - - - -
Message:  Node Background Investigation added to tree.


- - - - - - - - - - - - - - - - - - - - - - - - - - - - - - - - - - - - - - - - - -
   Please enter next command:

down

   Which node do you wish to descend from?
   Please enter a number between 1 and 2.

2

   To descend the tree you must create a new node.
   Name for this node?

In-house Investigators
```

Figure 5.16 Finishing out one subtree (Part 1). This figure (Part 1 of 6 parts) shows the completion of the "Personnel Security" subtree of the tree shown in Figure 5.7. The nodes can be added and estimates for their plausibilities of failure/loss, severity of failure/loss, etc. can be done in any order. The sequence in the 6 parts of this figure show *one* possible order.

```
  1. In-house Investigators                             $        down       print
                                                        !        end        save
                                                        ?        estimate   set
                                                        add      help       show
                                                        analyze  name       status
                                                        delete   new        up
- - - - - - - - - - - - - - - - - - - - - - - - - - - - - - - - - - - - - - - - - -
Message:  Node In-house Investigators added to tree.


- - - - - - - - - - - - - - - - - - - - - - - - - - - - - - - - - - - - - - - - - -
   Please enter next command:

add

   Name for this node:

Investigation Firm
```

Figure 5.16 Finishing out one subtree (Part 2). This figure (Part 2 of 6 parts) shows the completion of the "Personnel Security" subtree.

```
    1.  In-house Investigators                    $        down       print
    2.  Investigation Firm                        !        end        save
                                                  ?        estimate   set
                                                  add      help       show
                                                  analyze  name       status
                                                  delete   new        up
    -------------------------------------------------------------------------
    Message:  Node Investigation Firm added to tree.


    -------------------------------------------------------------------------
      Please enter next command:

    estimate

      Which node do you wish to enter estimates for?
      Please enter a number between 1 and 2.

    1

      Enter fuzzy likelyhood of the failure of this node: High
      Enter fuzzy confidence of your prediction: Very Low
      Enter fuzzy severity of the failure of this node: Extremely High
```

Figure 5.16 Finishing out one subtree (Part 3). This figure (Part 3 of 6 parts) shows the completion of the "Personnel Security" subtree.

```
    1.  In-house Investigators                    $        down       print
    2.  Investigation Firm                        !        end        save
                                                  ?        estimate   set
                                                  add      help       show
                                                  analyze  name       status
                                                  delete   new        up
    -------------------------------------------------------------------------



    -------------------------------------------------------------------------
      Please enter next command:

    estimate

      Which node do you wish to enter estimates for?
      Please enter a number between 1 and 2.

    2


      Enter fuzzy likelyhood of the failure of this node: Extremely Low
      Enter fuzzy confidence of your prediction: Rather High
      Enter fuzzy severity of the failure of this node: Extremely High
```

Figure 5.16 Finishing out one subtree (Part 4). This figure (Part 4 of 6 parts) shows the completion of the "Personnel Security" subtree.

```
 1. In-house Investigators          $        down        print
 2. Investigation Firm              !        end         save
                                    ?        estimate    set
                                    add      help        show
                                    analyze  name        status
                                    delete   new         up
---------------------------------------------------------------------



---------------------------------------------------------------------

    Please enter next command:

up
```

Figure 5.16 Finishing out one subtree (Part 5). This figure (Part 5 of 6 parts) shows the completion of the "Personnel Security" subtree.

```
 1. Polygraph                       $        down        print
 2. Background Investigation        !        end         save
                                    ?        estimate    set
                                    add      help        show
                                    analyze  name        status
                                    delete   new         up
---------------------------------------------------------------------



---------------------------------------------------------------------

    Please enter next command:

estimate

    Which node do you wish to enter estimates for?
    Please enter a number between 1 and 2.

2

    Enter fuzzy weight of this node: Low
    Enter fuzzy confidence of your prediction: Medium
```

Figure 5.16 Finishing out one subtree (Part 6). This figure (Part 6 or 6 parts) shows the completion of the "Personnel Security" subtree.

```
1. Polygraph                              $       down      print
2. Background Investigation               !       end       save
                                          ?       estimate  set
                                          add     help      show
                                          analyze name      status
                                          delete  new       up
-----------------------------------------------------------------------


-----------------------------------------------------------------------
   Please enter next command:

up



```

Figure 5.17 Ascending the tree from the third to the second level.

```
1. Physical Security                      $       down      print
2. Software Security                      !       end       save
3. Personnel Security                     ?       estimate  set
                                          add     help      show
                                          analyze name      status
                                          delete  new       up
-----------------------------------------------------------------------


-----------------------------------------------------------------------
   Please enter next command:

down

   To descend the tree you must create a new node.
   Name for this node?

Operating System



```

Figure 5.18 Descending from the second to the third level. At this point, the user is about to build the "Software Security" subtree.

```
   1. Operating System                          $        down        print
                                                 !        end         save
                                                 ?        estimate    set
                                                 add      help        show
                                                 analyze  name        status
                                                 delete   new         up
------------------------------------------------------------------------------
Message: Node Operating System added to tree.


------------------------------------------------------------------------------
   Please enter next command:

add

   Name for this node?

Utilities



```

Figure 5.19 Creating the "Software Security" subtree. (Part 1 of 2)

```
   1. Operating System                          $        down        print
   2. Utilities                                  !        end         save
                                                 ?        estimate    set
                                                 add      help        show
                                                 analyze  name        status
                                                 delete   new         up
------------------------------------------------------------------------------
Message: Node Utilities added to tree.


------------------------------------------------------------------------------
   Please enter next command:

down

   To descend the tree you must create a new node.
   Name for this node?

In-House



```

Figure 5.19 Creating the "Software Security" subtree. (Part 2 of 2)

Name	Weight	Confidence	Likelihood	Severity
Total System				
	--	Currently at this level		
Physical Security	L to M	High		
Badges		M to H	M to H	Extre. High
Cipher Lock		Low	Rather High	High
24-Hour Guard		Medium	Very Low	Very High
Software Security	High	M to H		
Operating System	Extre. High	High		
Logon Passwords		Very Low	High to Very High	Very High
File Access		Medium	Low	Very High
Super User Access		Rather High	Very Low	Extre. High
Utilities	Extre. High	Medium		
In-House		Medium	Low	High
Contractor		L to M	L to M	Very High
Personnel Security	Extre. High	Extre. High		
Polygraph		M to H	M to H	Extre. Low
Background Investigation	High	High		
In-House Investigators		High	Rather High	Extre. High
Investigation Firm		High	Very Low	Extre. High

Please push return to continue:

Figure 5.20 The result of the **print** command for the entire tree. Note that only the natural language estimates that will actually be used in the subsequent computations are shown (e.g., only weight and confidence are shown for non-terminal nodes). If the tree did not fit on one screen, the user would be instructed to push "return" to see the remainder of the listing.

```
    1. Total System                         $        down      print
                                            !        end       save
                                            ?        estimate  set
                                           add       help      show
                                           analyze   name      status
                                           delete    new       up
    ------------------------------------------------------------------------



    ------------------------------------------------------------------------
     Please enter next command:

  analyze




```

Figure 5.21 Invoking the **analyze** command.

```
    1. Total System                         $        down      print
                                            !        end       save
                                            ?        estimate  set
                                           add       help      show
                                           analyze   name      status
                                           delete    new       up
    ------------------------------------------------------------------------



    ------------------------------------------------------------------------
     The analysis of the tree can be done with:
          1)  Fuzzy algorithms
          2)  Numeric algorithms

     Please enter a number between 1 and 2.

  1

     Tree Total System evaluates to Fairly Low to Medium
     Would you like to see a print of the tree?

  No
```

Figure 5.22 Using the **analyze** command.

```
1. Total System                              $        down      print
                                             !        end       save
                                             ?        estimate  set
                                             add      help      show
                                             analyze  name      status
                                             delete   new       up
----------------------------------------------------------------------


----------------------------------------------------------------------
Please enter next command:

save

   File name for this tree to be saved in?

EXAMPLE1
```

Figure 5.23 Saving the result of an FRA session.

```
1. Total System                              $        down      print
                                             !        end       save
                                             ?        estimate  set
                                             add      help      show
                                             analyze  name      status
                                             delete   new       up
----------------------------------------------------------------------


----------------------------------------------------------------------
   Please enter next command:

end

   FRA terminating
```

Figure 5.24 Terminating an FRA session.

Continuing in this manner the entire tree of Figure 5.8 is constructed within the FRA framework. Figure 5.20 shows the results of a **print** command listing all the nodes of the tree together with their natural language estimates in an indented format.

At this point the user is ready to compute the risk associated with the entire tree. The results of the **analyze** command are shown in Figure 5.21 and Figure 5.22.

Since this tree structure represents the first approximation of a detailed description of the user's installation, the results are saved in a file for later modification, with the interaction sequence shown in Figure 5.23.

The user then terminates the FRA session as shown in Figure 5.24.

Thus, we see that the FRA offers a quick and easy method for the evaluation of the risk of a system that can be decomposed hierarchically. The FRA is an evaluation method that is natural and simple to use—so much so that the evaluation can be carried out by a non-expert risk analyst. Because of its ease of use, the FRA can be used even for the evaluation of hypothetical situations, as a type of "what if" analytic aid, allowing the evaluation of proposed situations without the expenditure of large amounts of resources or time.

Chapter 6

FUTURE RESEARCH

There are a number of avenues available for the improvement and/or extension of the Fuzzy Risk Analyzer. One that is currently being researched is the possibility of allowing the user to query the fuzzy model constructed by the FRA for a given system. While queries of the form "What individual component contributed most heavily to the risk of this node?" are the most requested queries, others are also contemplated. Being able to query the system in this fashion is not unlike the artificial intelligence systems that allow the user to investigate the "reasoning" behind the system responses. Though nothing so elaborate is currently planned for the FRA, it is felt that even this moderate query capability of determining the greatest contributor, the least, the most risky sub-system, etc. will greatly aid the practicing risk analyst. An algorithm for achieving this is presented in Meadows, [1981].

Another area for future research that is being examined is algorithm improvement, most noticeably in the calculation of the fuzzy weighted mean and in the final mapping from the calculated fuzzy set back to an appropriate natural language expression. It is not at all clear to all the FRA researchers that Clements' definition of the fuzzy weighted mean [Clements, 1977] truly captures the essence of the arithmetic mean or that his scheme is computationally efficient. Much work of the current research team is now examining the theoretical and computational aspects of this definition. The other algorithmic improvement being contemplated is the replacement of the Best Fit method for the fuzzy-set-to-natural-language-expression mapping. Both the method of Successive Approximation and the method of Piecewise Decomposition are being investigated as well as one novel approach. Both the Successive Approximation and the Piecewise Decomposition methods take as input one fuzzy set and produce as output one natural language expression. The FRA allows another dimension, the reliability estimate. Is it not reasonable that this reliability estimate could be used as a fuzzy output as well as a fuzzy input? As an output value, the reliability estimate could measure, for example, the proximity of the computed fuzzy set to the fuzzy definition of the closest natural language expression—sort of the system's confidence in its own approximation. Isn't it possible that even the closest fuzzy set might still be rather far away and shouldn't the user be made aware of this fact if it occurs?

Also, there are the somewhat controversial operations of normalization and convex closure. In the work of other researchers, these operations were mandatory in order for the ultimate fuzzy-set-to-natural-language mapping to be possible. But taking the convex closure can greatly increase the degree of membership of some components of a fuzzy set. Consider the fuzzy set shown in Figure 6.1 (taken from Clements, [1977]). Both the fuzzy set and its convex closure are shown in that figure—the fuzzy set could be described by the natural language expression 'ABOUT 2 *OR* ABOUT 8' while the convex closure would be better described by 'ABOUT 2 *TO* ABOUT 8). Clearly, these are quite different expressions and they do not present identical images to the end user. Forcing convexity has increased the degree of membership of 5, for example, in the fuzzy set depicted in Figure 6.1 from a zero degree of membership to one of complete membership! If this has to be done, perhaps the confidence parameter is the place to record this fact for the analyst's later use. Similarly, normalization artificially increases the degree of membership of all the elements of the fuzzy set. If the highest degree of membership in the set is .46, isn't this significant in later mapping this set back to the natural language expression? Perhaps allowing

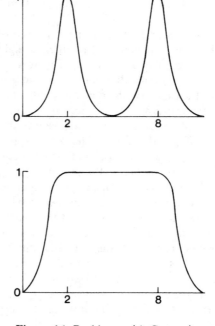

Figure 6.1 Problems with Convexity.

non-normalized primary terms as well as non-normalized final results will provide another "dimension" with which to better model the user's natural language input. Or perhaps normalization, if it is really necessary, should be accompanied by a decrease (whatever that means for a fuzzy set) in the fuzzy set measuring the *system's* confidence in *its* own estimate! These questions deserve a thorough theoretical and practical examination and such a study is now planned.

We have seen that some psychological research suggests alternate definitions for some fuzzy operations as well as for the modeling of some hedges and we will discuss those results later in this section. From strictly a technical point of view some mathematicians have also advanced new definitions of the basic fuzzy operations [Schefe, 1980], [Koksalan and Dagli, 1981]. The Schefe modifications are based on a desire to preserve certain logical "truths" from ordinary two-valued logic and the Koksalan and Dagli modifications were empirically chosen to improve their fuzzy model. Some thought should be given to experimenting with these notions, though any such modifications would perhaps result in a loss of the firm mathematical foundation for much of our work.

The above research topics for the FRA are essentially theoretical (or at least technical) questions dealing with fuzzy set theory and its computational applications. There is another, entirely different aspect to the FRA: its degree of correlation with the way real people use natural language ratings and with the way real risk analysts do their job. It appears clear that much of the FRA research in the near future will center on these psycholinguistic and managerial science questions. Should the set of hedges be enlarged? To include what new hedges from the seemingly unbounded set of appropriate English words? Or, rather, is the set of hedges now used sufficient, but perhaps inadequately modeled? As we have remarked earlier, researchers have found that our modeling of the hedge 'very' (as the CON operator) is only *one* of two ways that people actually use that word [Hersh and Caramazza, 1976], [Lakoff, 1973], [Oden, 1977], [Macvicar-Whelen, 1978]. Zadeh himself has acknowledged the vast complexity of the modeling of hedges:

It should be emphasized, however, that these representations are intended mainly to illustrate the approach rather than to provide accurate definitions of the hedges in question. Furthermore, it must be underscored that our analysis and its conclusions are tentative in nature and may require modification in later work [Zadeh, 1972].

Another researcher states,

(In defining the meanings for hedges) Zadeh happened to use squares, square roots, and factors of two. However, he does not intend those exact numbers to be taken seriously. What he does intend to be taken seriously is the kinds of effects these functions have on the curve. Whether 3 or 1.745 would be better numbers than 2 in such functions is irrelevant, so long as CON pulls the curve in, DIL spreads it out, and INT heightens contrasts... [Lakoff, 1973].

While almost all researchers agree that the modeling of hedges is complex, this does not necessarily extend to the other linguistic elements we have modeled. Wenstop analyzed the same complex natural language expressions with different semantic definitions for the primary terms and found no appreciable differences in the resulting semantics of the expressions. Indeed,

> the exact form of the internal definition of primary terms matters little, as long as they do not violate obvious common sense principles [Wenstop, 1979].

Clearly there is much work to be done here. With regard to the primary terms, the robustness of the fuzzy definitions should be verified for the domain of risk analysis. With regard to the hedges, perhaps the hedge modeling should employ more context-sensitivity, or make more use of the psychological literature. Some have suggested that a more general definition of the fuzzy sets used to model natural language expressions would improve their correlation with the way people use such expressions. One extension that is possible is to allow the characteristic functions of the fuzzy sets to take their values not in [0, 1], but in a mathematically more abstract entity like a lattice. The mathematical properties of a distributive lattice, for example, may make it possible to model natural language expressions without imposing additional structure (like orderings) on those expressions [Kaufmann, 1977]. In the long run, it may be psychological/ managerial science studies like Nagy and Hoffman, [1981] that may provide the bulk of the data for the improvement of the user interface of the FRA—data that would in turn require some changes in the behind-the-scenes processing. The conclusions of that pilot study deserve further investigation.

One final area that may lead to an improvement to the current FRA is in the input and output modes now used. Currently the FRA accepts a rigidly format-ted alphanumeric input hierarchically describing the system to be analyzed and then produces an alphanumeric output that is somewhat hard to decipher (in the opinion of this author). Like almost every area of applied computer science from office automation to process control to software development, the FRA may benefit from the use of computer graphics to facilitate the information transfer from man to machine. Even without much imagination one can envision both graphical input and output for the FRA that are vastly easier to use than the current system and also less prone to error.

Probably the best method of providing a new user interface for the FRA is to make use of recent work in the use of high resolution bit-mapped graphics displays to provide interfaces that are easy to learn and use. [1,2,3] In this type of

---

[1]Teitelman, W., A Display Oriented Programmer's Assistant, Technical Report CSL-77-3, Xerox Palo Alto Research Centers, (8 March 1977); also published in the *International Journal of Man-Machine Studies*, vol. 11, (1978), 157-187.

[2]Smith, David C., Charles Irby, Ralph Kimball, Bill Verplank and Eric Harslem, Designing the STAR User Interface, *BYTE*, (April 1982), 242-282.

interface, the user interacts with a number of variable-size, pop-up windows that can quickly be made to appear and disappear on the screen. The user's mode of operation is typically one of *selection* of a visible entity. In the case of the FRA, these entities would include *that* node of the tree or *this* fuzzy weight. A new user interface for the FRA, specifically constructed in the spirit and style of this type of user interface, would be a tremendous step forward in making the capabilities of the FRA more easily used by a wider audience. While such an interface would require computational resources than are presently unavailable in $5,000 or $10,000 personal computers, many computer scientists believe these resources will not be beyond the power of a $5,000 or $10,000 personal computer in the near future. A first attempt at this type of user interface is presented in the following pages. This is, at present, only a design; no working system is currently available.

In this new user interface for the FRA, the user interacts directly with a graphical representation of the tree to be analyzed. For example, the user inserts a new node by merely *pointing to* a blank area on the CRT. A number of actions can be performed by pointing directly at a node. The subtree of which that node is the head can be analyzed; the current estimate of the plausibility of failure/loss of the node (i.e., the natural language expression denoting the risk value that node has to its parent node), the weight estimate of that node with respect to the other nodes, the reliability estimate in the plausibility, severity, and weight values, and the textual description of the node can all be changed; the node can be deleted entirely. With the single exception of changing the textual description of the node, the user never has to type anything. Commands (like **Analyze, Change Severity, Change Weight**, etc.) are selected from windows that pop up on the screen when required and then disappear when no longer needed. Even the natural language expressions used for the plausibility, severity, weight, and reliability estimates are *selected* rather than *entered*, again via pop-up windows. The following description of the interface deals first with the construction of the tree diagram, then with the modification of the various natural language estimates, and lastly with the operation of the commands related to the tree and its subtrees. In actual practice, however, the user can perform these actions in any order.

The goals of an interface of this type include (ranging from the general to the specific):

- To make the normally invisible and abstract components of the user's model of the system visible and concrete,
- To make the system modeless ("A mode of an interactive computer system is a state of the user interface that lasts for a period of time, is not associated

---

[3]Goldberg, Adele, and David Robson, *SmallTalk: The Language and Implementation*, (Reading, Ma: Addison-Wesley), 1983.

with any particular object, and has no role other than to place an interpretation on operator input"[4]),

- To make the system easily accessible to the infrequent user, eliminating the need for extensive re-training, i.e., make the system hard to forget,
- To provide the user with immediate results of the risk analysis, thereby providing the capability for more "what if" exploratory analysis,
- To make the system usable by a novice risk analyst with little or no prior experience using the FRA, after less than one hour of training,
- To overcome the interference problems associated with pseudo-natural language systems. (There are currently no *full* natural language systems. Systems that provide a natural language-like interface suffer from *interference* when the user has difficulty remembering exactly what subset of natural language is correctly processed by the system. For the FRA specifically, interference could occur if the user couldn't remember if EXTREMELY was a hedge of the FRA or not.), and
- To provide a *"What-you-see-is-what-you-get"* image of the FRA tree.

Construction of the Tree

Let us assume that the user wished to construct and analyze the risk for the situation first presented in Figure 5.7. When the FRA is started in such a situation (i.e., the analysis of a new scenario as opposed to the modification to an existing analysis), the user is presented with the display shown in Figure 6.2. Notice that a head node is automatically present, since use of the FRA presupposes a hierarchical tree structure with a single head node. Notice, too, that the head node is shaded. (The significance of this shading will be shown later.) This figure and most of the ones following depict what the end user would actually see at each step of the risk analysis of this scenario using the FRA.

In Figure 6.3 the user indicates the approximate position of one of the descendants of the head node, using perhaps a flexible graphic input device like a mouse or a joystick, rather than the more common, but inflexible, cursor step keys.[5]).

Figures 6.4, 6.5, and 6.6 show the system's placement of a new node and another descendant of the head node.

In order to place nodes at the next level (the third level of the tree), the user selects one of the two descendants with the cursor. Figure 6.7 shows the selection of the rightmost descendant of the head node. This node now takes on the shaded pattern denoting the current node to which descendants are appended and Figure 6.8 shows the result of appending two new nodes below this current node.

---

[4]Tesler, Larry, as quoted in "Designing the STAR User Interface", David C. Smith, Charles Irby, Ralph Kimball, Bill Verplank and Eric Harslem, *BYTE*, (April 1982), 242–282, but also see Tesler's article, "The Smalltalk Environment", *BYTE*, (August, 1981), 90–147.

[5]Card, Stuart K., William K. English, and Betty Burr, Evaluation of Mouse, Rate-Controlled Isometric Joystick, Step Keys, and Text Keys for Text Selection on a CRT, *Ergonomics*, vol. 21, (1978), 601–613.

Figure 6.2 The FRA is started in the situation in which the user wishes to construct a new scenario to be analyzed. The heavy rectangle indicates the border of the graphics display that is the key element in this new user interface for the FRA.

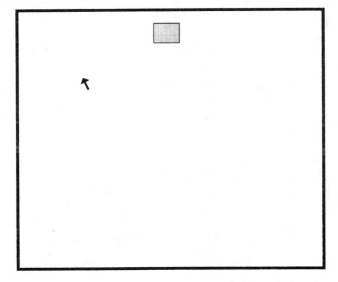

Figure 6.3 Using a two-dimensional graphic input device, the user indicates the approximate placement of a descendant node to the current head node. By using only approximate placement the user can indicate the positioning of nodes relative to each other while leaving the aesthetic display of the final tree to the FRA.

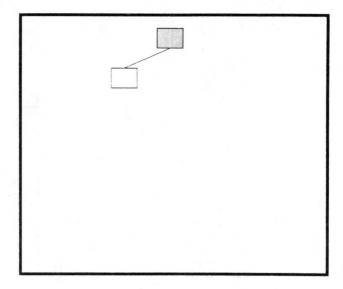

Figure 6.4 The addition of a new node to the tree.

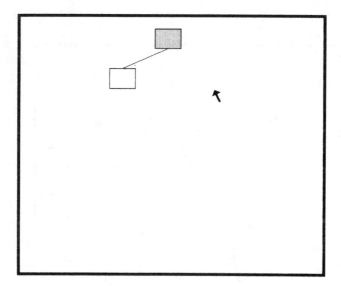

Figure 6.5 Indicating the position of a new descendant node.

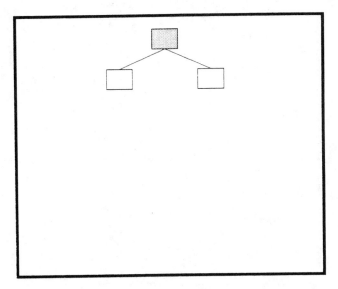

Figure 6.6 Placement of the new node. Notice that even though the user's input for the position of these two nodes was not exactly the same distance from the head node, the resulting tree is graphically balanced and symmetric about the head node.

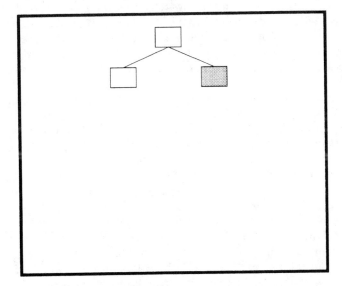

Figure 6.7 Changing the current node. The current node is the node to which new nodes are attached. Notice that the user is selecting a visible entity on the screen for this operation—*not* directly manipulating the invisible internal computer representations or working with somewhat confusing tree node numbering schemes.

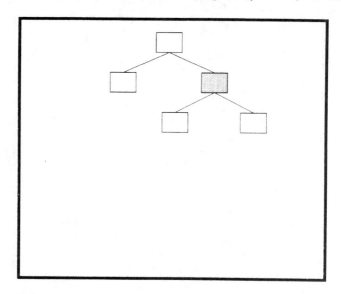

Figure 6.8 The addition of two new nodes. To position these new nodes, the user only indicated the approximate positions below the current node.

In order to append a new node below any node on the screen, the user merely has to select that node (thus, making that node the current node) and then indicate the position of the descendant. This can be done for any existing node. Thus, the user can easily construct the nodes of the tree in any order, relying on the placement and graphical interconnections to indicate the tree structure required for his analysis. For example, even though the user has just added two nodes at the third level of the tree, he could add an additional descendant to the head node by selecting it and then indicating an approximate position as is shown in Figures 6.9 and 6.10. Note that this may result in the adjustment of the positions of many nodes as is shown in Figure 6.11. This use of only approximate positioning allows, for example, the user to indicate that a new node should be positioned between two existing nodes (where "between" means between on a left to right scan on one level of the tree), *without* being concerned about the actual formatting of the image of the tree.

Continuing in this manner, the entire tree structure of Figure 5.7 can be entered by the user with the final result shown in Figure 6.12. Note that some parts of the tree are temporarily not visible on the screen. Mechanisms enabling the user to "pan" around the tree exist and will be dealt with in the section dealing with operations on the tree and its subtrees. In addition, the next two sections do not show reduced sketches of the actual screen images, but rather enlarged or actual size sketches and, thus, these enlarged sketches are able to show in detail the

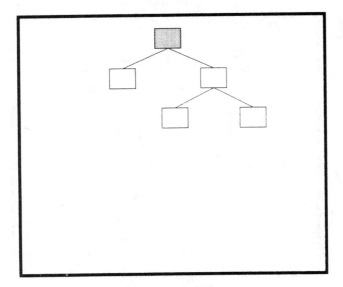

Figure 6.9 Selection of the head node in order to insert a new node at level two.

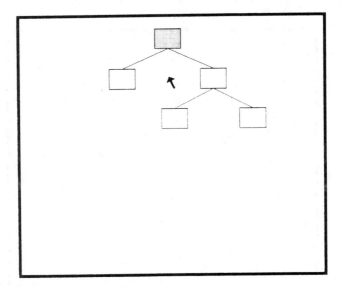

Figure 6.10 Indicating the approximate position of the new node.

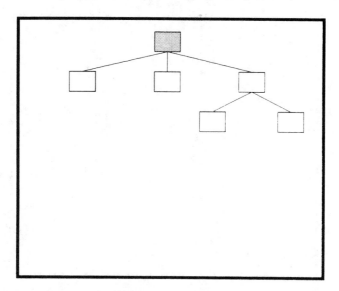

Figure 6.11　Insertion of the new node. Note that the image of the entire second level (and, thus, all the following levels) of the tree have "spread out" in order to accommodate this new node.

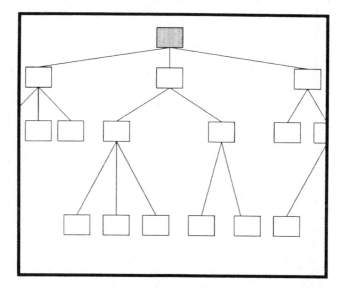

Figure 6.12　The total tree structure of Figure 5.7 entered using the new graphics interface.

internal structure of the individual nodes, where the current values for the node's plausibility of failure/loss, severity of failure/loss, relative weight, and reliability estimates can be seen.

Assigning Natural Language Expressions

Properties are values temporarily associated with a particular entity. In this proposed user interface for the FRA, the plausibility of failure/loss, severity of failure/loss, relative weight, and reliability estimates are all considered to be properties of the node, in much the same way that a text string has properties of font, size, italics or bold face, or a line has the properties of being solid, dashed, or dotted. Merely changing a line from dotted to dashed does not affect the existence of the line, or its position. Changing the weight of a particular node in the FRA does not delete the node, change its level in the tree, or alter the surrounding nodes in any way.

The user changes the value of the estimates for a node's plausibility, severity, weight, or reliability through interaction with that node's appropriate *property sheet*, a pop-up window that allows the selection of the natural language expressions which are the values of these estimates. (Figure 6.13 shows the particular property sheet for weight.)

The property sheet consists of two major portions: the menu portion shown with a gray background, and the selection portion shown with a white background. The menu portion allows the user to select commands associated with the property sheet. Note that until the property sheet is displayed there is no reason for the user to issue any of these commands. There is also no need for him to *remember* them during his general operations with the FRA. These particular commands (and many others in different situations) are displayed whenever the user could make meaningful use of them, hence, all he need do is select the desired command from the ones he is shown. This hiding of information until it is needed by the user is called *progressive disclosure* and is a key feature of making a system easy for the beginner to learn, and the casual user to remember. The **?** command on the menu portion of the property sheet displays a help sheet that explains the operations of this particular property sheet—a context-sensitive help button. The **Done** command updates the property of the affected node to whatever values the user has set on the property sheet. The **Default** command sets the property sheet values to the system default, thus providing the novice with a standard action when he is undecided. The **Reset** command sets the property sheet back to the values it had before it was displayed.

The bottom half of the property sheet of Figure 6.13, the selection portion, allows the user to select the particular natural language expression for the weight of a node. The user selects the combination of hedges and primary terms desired by touching the appropriate words with the cursor. Those combinations of

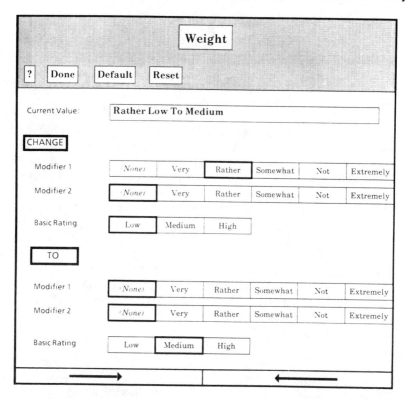

Figure 6.13 The property sheet for weight of the new graphics interface. Note that this figure shows the property sheet at several times normal size.

hedges and primary terms that are not in the grammar of the FRA language are not selectable, e.g., were the user to select the primary term "MEDIUM", the two rows of hedges modifying that primary term would disappear, since expressions like "EXTREMELY NOT MEDIUM" and "NOT VERY MEDIUM" are not reasonable expressions. Thus, the property sheet interface neatly overcomes the interference problem associated with many other natural language-like systems. The user does not have to *remember* which natural language expressions are correctly processed by the FRA and which are not: the ones that are, are the only ones he can choose. There is also an additional benefit to this feature of selection via property sheet for the natural language expressions. When changes are made to the grammar that the FRA processes, for example, by adding new hedges or allowing more complex combinations of hedges and primary terms, no re-training of users is required. When a property sheet appears, it will merely present, either explicitly or implicitly, additional options. Such extension ease is not present when the user must remember and type in the natural language expressions. In such a case the implementer would have to publicize among all the users that, for example, the hedge BARELY was now available.

At first glance it might seem that there is only room on the property sheet for about five hedge choices and that any extension beyond this would require enlarging the property sheet, thereby obliterating, albeit only for a short time, more of the FRA tree. The two arrows at the bottom of the property sheet present a solution to the problem of additional hedges that does not require the enlargement of the property sheet. These arrows, called scroll arrows, allow the user to horizontally scroll the contents to the property sheet. Figure 6.14 shows the result of scrolling the weight property sheet of Figure 6.13 to the left, a consequence of the user touching the left pointing arrow with the cursor.

In this new user interface for the FRA the natural language estimates of individual nodes are always visible on the graphics screen. Individual nodes of the tree have the structure shown in Figure 6.15. In this way, the estimates are always visible and thus are concrete properties associated with the node.

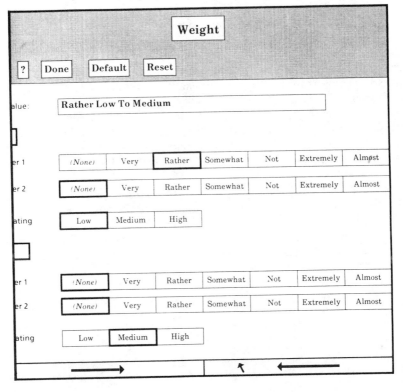

Figure 6.14 The property sheet for weight shifted slightly to the left through the use of the left pointing scroll bar.

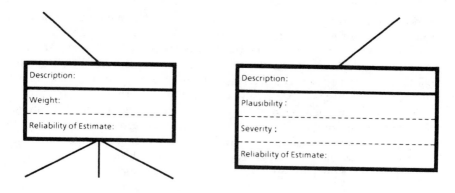

Node with descendants   **Node without descendants**

Figure 6.15 Node appearances for the new FRA user interface.

The user changes the natural language estimates for a given node by first selecting the node with the cursor and then indicating which of the estimates he wishes to change (through the use, for example, of buttons labelled "Plausibility," "Severity," "Weight," and "Reliability"). A property sheet then appears on the screen, temporarily overlaying a portion of the FRA tree. Figure 6.16 shows a portion of the screen containing the selected node and its Weight property sheet. Figures 6.17 through 6.24 show the interaction sequence as the user changes the weight of the "Software Security" node from "Rather High" to "Medium to Not Extremely High."

The plausibility of failure/loss, severity of failure/loss, relative weight, and reliability estimates for any node are set in exactly the same manner as Figures 6.15 through 6.24 depict for the relative weight estimate of the "Software Security" node. While this may seem to be a somewhat slow and time-consuming procedure from an observation of these static figures, it is not when dynamically presented. This is especially true if the time to display any given property sheet is less than one or two seconds. (The only existing system which uses a user interface with property sheets, the Xerox Star Professional Workstation,[6] takes

---

[6]The Xerox Star user interface represents a revolutionary advance in the design of man-machine dialogs and has *heavily* influenced the author in the design of this new user interface for the FRA. Descriptions of the Star user interface as well as independent reviews of the result can be found in the following references:

Smith, David C., Charles Irby, Ralph Kimball, and Eric Harslem, The Star User Interface: An Overview, *Proceedings of the 1982 NCC*, AFIPS Press.

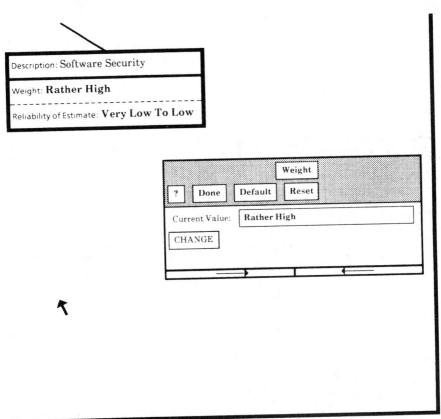

Figure 6.16 The Weight property sheet for the node "Software Security." If the user wishes to change the natural language estimate for the weight of this node, he must toggle the "CHANGE" box in the property sheet.
(Note that in this and the following figures, only a portion of the screen is depicted.)

Smith, David C., Charles Irby, Ralph Kimball, Bill Verplank and Eric Harslem, Designing the STAR User Interface, *BYTE*, (April 1982), 242-282.

Purvy, Robert, Jerry Farrell, and Paul Klose, The Design of Star's Records Processing, *Proceedings Supplement of the SIGOA Conference on Office Automation Systems,* Philadelphia, Penn., (21-23 June 1982), 1-12.

Lipkie, Daniel E., Steven R. Evans, John K. Newlin, and Robert Weissman, Star Graphics: An Object-Oriented Implementation, *Computer Graphics*, vol. 16, no. 3, (July 1982), 115-124.

Meyrowitz, Norman, and Andries vanDam, Interactive Editing Systems, *Computing Surveys*, vol. 14, no. 3, (September 1982), 321-416.

Furuta, Richard, Jeffrey Scofield, and Alan Shaw, Document Formatting Systems: Survey, Concepts, and Issues, *Computing Surveys*, vol. 14, no. 3, (September 1982), 417-472.

Seybold, Jonathan, Xerox's Star, in The Seybold Report, Media, Penn.: Seybold Publications, vol. 10, no. 16, (27 April 1981).

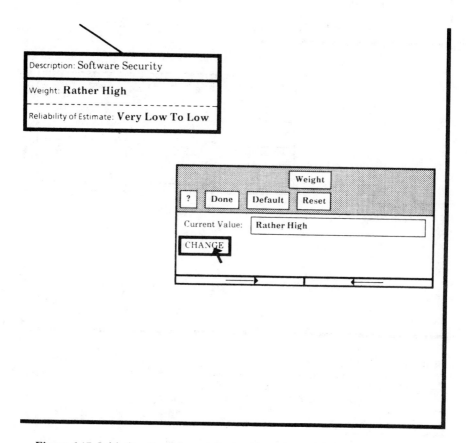

Figure 6.17 Initiating the action to change the weight of the "Software Security" node.

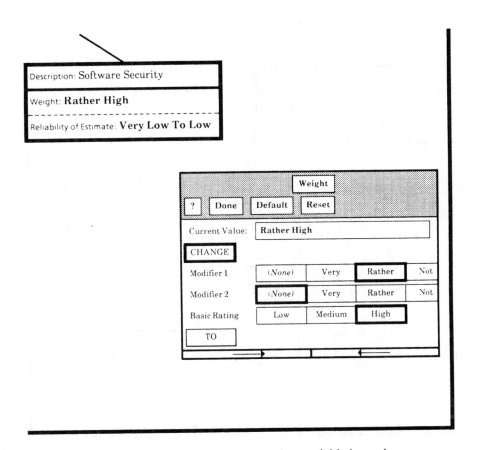

Figure 6.18 The new choices offered to the user initiating a change.

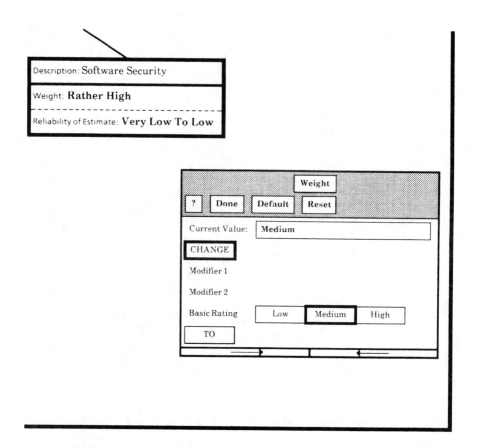

Figure 6.19 The result of toggling the Medium basic rating. Note that one and only one of the primary terms on a given Basic Rating line may be selected at one time. Also note that since natural language expressions like "VERY MEDIUM," "SOMEWHAT NOT MEDIUM," etc. are of dubious value, the property sheet does not allow the selection of any hedges when the primary term "MEDIUM" is chosen.

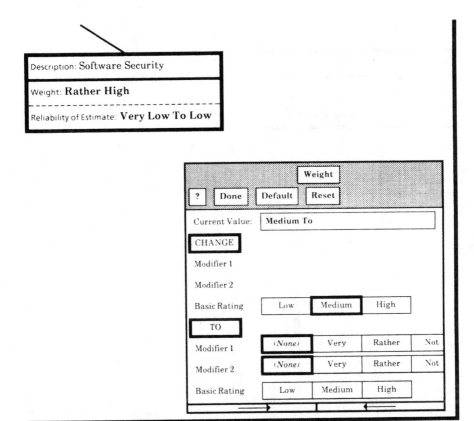

Figure 6.20 After selection of the range "TO."

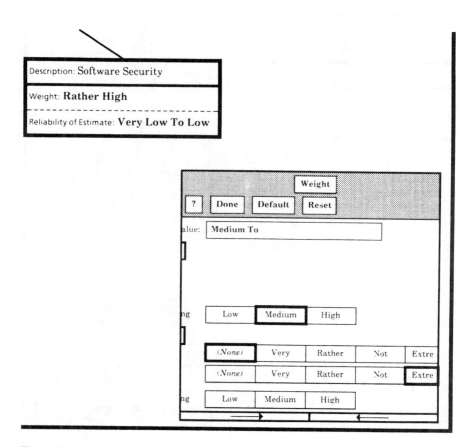

Figure 6.21 Scrolling the weight property sheet to the left in order to toggle the hedge "Extremely."

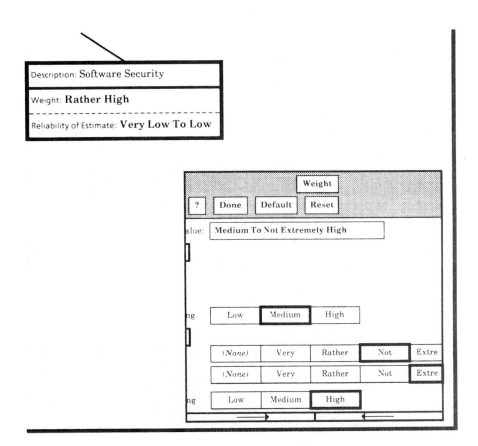

Description: Software Security

Weight: **Rather High**

Reliability of Estimate: **Very Low To Low**

Figure 6.22 After selection of "Not" and "High."

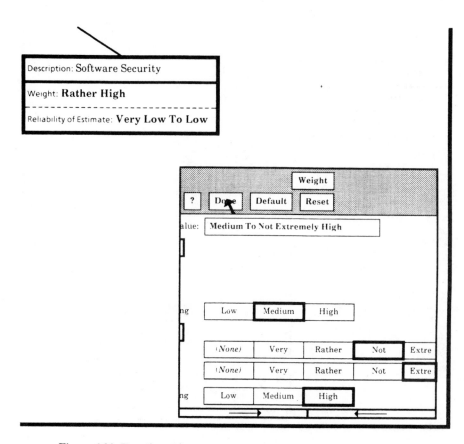

Figure 6.23 Toggling the property sheet "Done" command menu item.

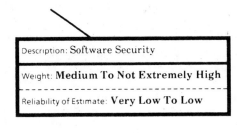

Description: Software Security

Weight: **Medium To Not Extremely High**

Reliability of Estimate: **Very Low To Low**

Figure 6.24 The resulting effect on the "Software Security" node. Note that the value of the weight estimate was not affected until the property sheet disappeared, and that the node *then* adjusted to the size of the largest natural language expression.

about 8 to 12 seconds to display a property sheet. The result is a property sheet mechanism that is usable but slightly annoying because of its slow speed.) Also this static presentation of the new FRA user interface has artificially separated the creation of the tree from the assignment of the natural language estimates. This separation was only present in order to make the explanation of this new interface easier to understand. In reality, the user would be able to create a node, set its various natural language values, create a couple of new nodes, set their values (in any order desired), et cetera. In this way we present a *modeless* interface to the FRA since the user is never in create mode, value mode, or analysis mode, but rather can easily structure the input and analysis of the desired scenario in a flexible, natural way. This modeless feature directly satisfies one of the design goals established for this new interface and indirectly contributes to the attainment of several others.

Operations on the Tree and Subtrees

At the "highest" level of this new FRA interface, the user sees the image shown in Figure 6.25. This figure shows exactly the screen image that the user really sees for all the operations in this new interface. This is in contrast to all the preceding figures, which were simplified to illustrate only the particular point being discussed about the interface at that time. One sees almost immediately a very strong resemblance between the supporting framework for the entire FRA tree (referred to as the FRA *window*) and the FRA property sheet, since both use the same menu portion at the top and the same horizontal scroll arrows at the bottom. In addition, the FRA window has vertical scroll arrows along the right side of the window, as can be seen in Figure 6.25. Thus, at this level of the interface, the user can scroll around the entire tree. Figure 6.26 shows the result of scrolling the tree of Figure 6.25 slightly to the right and Figure 6.27 the result of scrolling that tree slightly up. In this way the user can construct and access as large a tree as desired.

Also note that at this level of the new FRA interface there are fewer commands initially viewable to the viewer, compared with the alphanumeric interface. This is because many of the commands of the alphanumeric interface are simply not needed in the new interface. For example, the alphanumeric "up" and "down" commands that change the current level in the tree are not required here because this new interface does not have the notion of "current level"—the user can operate on any level just by touching any node at that level and then issuing the desired command.

In addition to scrolling about the tree, from the highest level of this new interface the user can calculate the fuzzy risk associated with the entire tree or with any of its subtrees, assess which of the subtrees of a given node contribute the greatest risk to that node, and merge any previously described tree with the

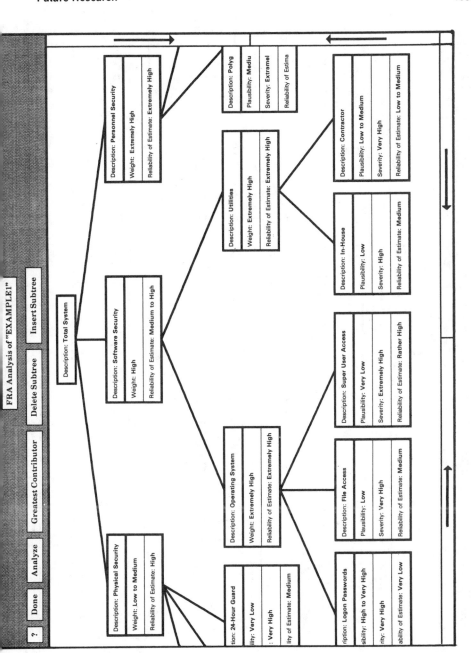

Figure 6.25 The entire screen image for the new user interface for the FRA. Note that the tree has a name (for future reference) shown at the top of the window menu. Note, too, the different size nodes.

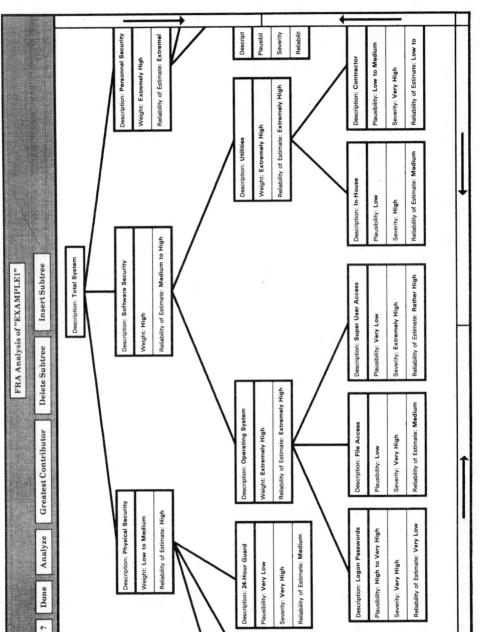

Figure 6.26 Scrolling the tree to the right using the right pointing scroll bar at the bottom of the window.

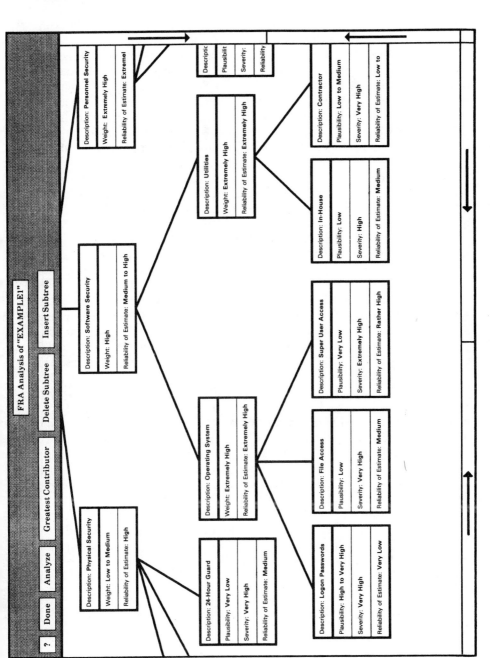

Figure 6.27 Scrolling the tree up using the upward pointing scroll bar at the bottom right of the window.

current tree and position it as any subtree within the current tree, thus allowing the modular composition of entire systems.

Suppose, for example, the user wishes to analyze the risk of the total system shown in Figure 6.25 (and first shown and analyzed in Figure 5.7.) The first step is to select the head node, as shown in Figure 6.28. Selecting the **Analyze** command in the tree window (as shown in Figure 6.29) causes the system to calculate the risk of the selected node. (In this case, the selected node is the head node and, thus, the risk calculated is the risk associated with the entire tree.) The results of this calculation are then placed in the value and reliability fields of the head node (as shown in Figure 6.30).

Figure 6.31 shows the result of using the **Greatest Contributor** command on the "Software Security" node. Note that the paths to the nodes which made the greatest contribution to the resulting risk of the "Software Security" node are highlighted. Exactly which of the descendants of a node contribute the greatest component to that node's risk is a function of the plausibility of failure/loss, severity of failure/loss, relative weight, and reliability estimates of all the descendants of that node. These values are in turn functions of the values of their descendants.

Figure 6.32 shows another, more detailed version of the Utilities sub-system constructed by a different analyst. To test the sensitivity of the analysis of the total risk of the entire system to the level of detail of the hierarchical description, we shall insert this new version as the Utilities subtree of the system under analysis, re-run the analysis, and see if the total system risk changes as a result of this finer breakdown of the Utilities subsystem. To do this we first delete this component (shown in Figures 6.33, 6.34, and 6.35 through the use of the **Delete Subtree** command). Figure 6.36 shows the query window which is generated upon invocation of the **Insert Subtree** command and Figures 6.37 and 6.38 show the operation of this window. Figure 6.39 shows the result of the insertion. In Figures 6.40 through 6.43 the weight estimate of the new "Utilities" node is added to the analysis and in Figures 6.44 through 6.46 the reliability estimate is also added. Figure 6.47 shows the result of analyzing the total risk of the entire tree which now includes this new component.

This new user interface for the FRA, if implemented, represents a significant amount of additional effort on top of that of implementing the fuzzy algorithms that are the essence of the FRA. Hopefully, such new "exterior packaging" for the FRA would make it an easier system to use and would encourage users to prepare more detailed and more accurate models of the total risk to which their system is subjected.

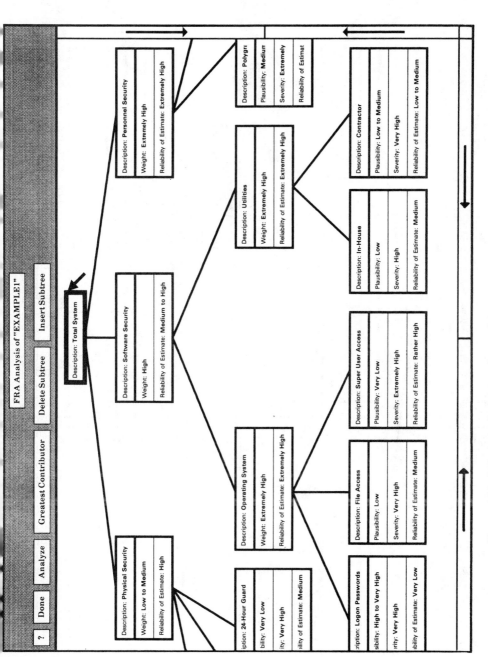

Figure 6.28 Selection of a node prior to using any one of the menu commands.

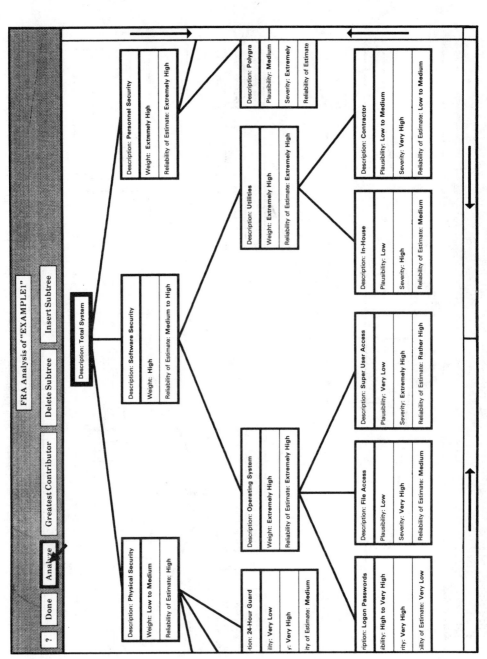

Figure 6.20 Selection of the Analyze command in the tree window

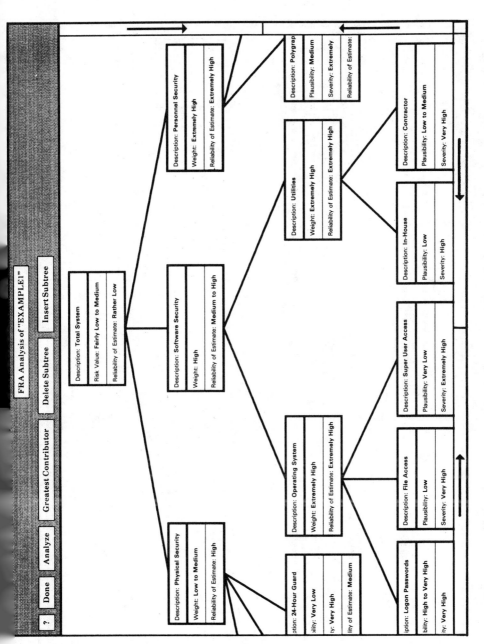

Figure 6.30 The result of the **Analyze** command. Notice that the value and reliability fields of the head node have been generated and filled in.

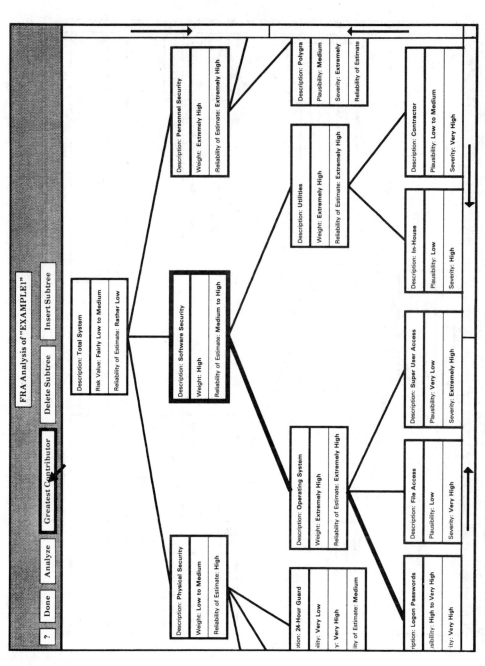

Figure 6.31 The result of the **Greatest Contributor** command on the "Software Security" node. Notice that the path to the greatest contributor is highlighted.

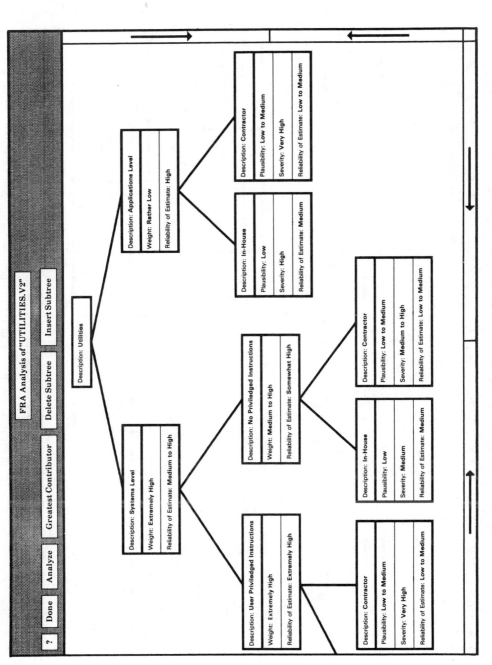

Figure 6.32 Another possible hierarchical breakdown of the Utilities component.

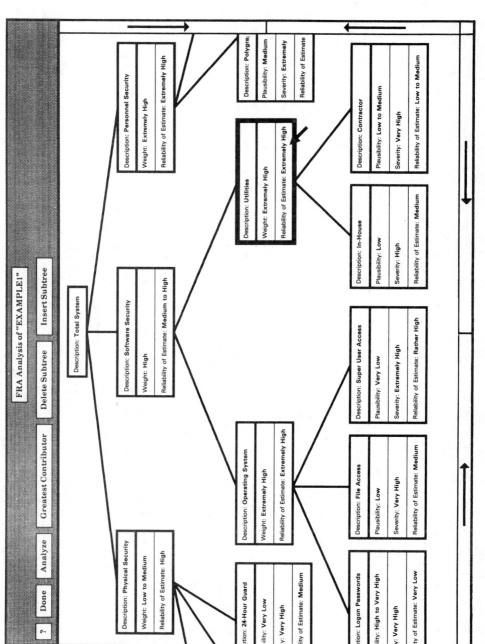

Figure 6.33 Selection of the Utilities subtree prior to deletion.

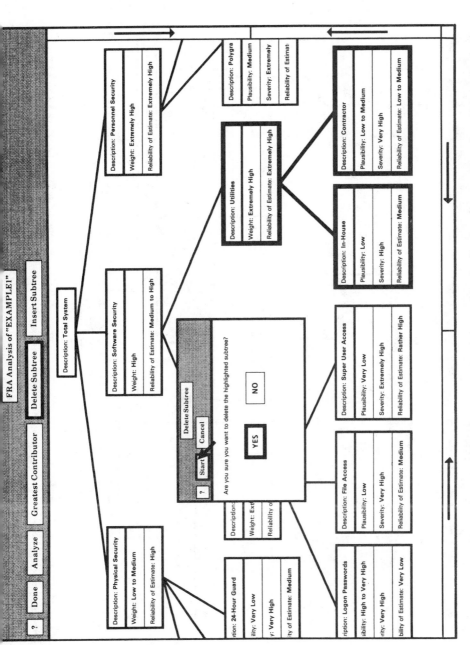

Figure 6.34 Invocation of the **Delete Subtree** command and the resulting feedback and query. Note that all the nodes that are to be deleted (all the nodes descended from the selected node) are highlighted and the user is then queried to make doubly certain that this deletion is the one desired.

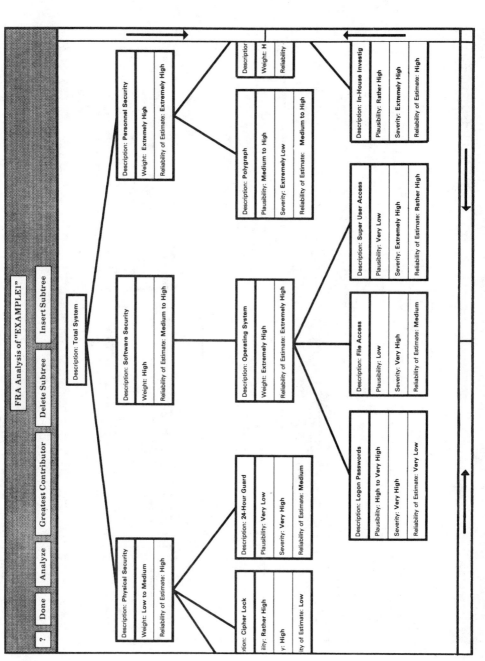

Figure 6.35 Following a positive response to the query generated by the **Delete Subtree** command. Notice that most of the

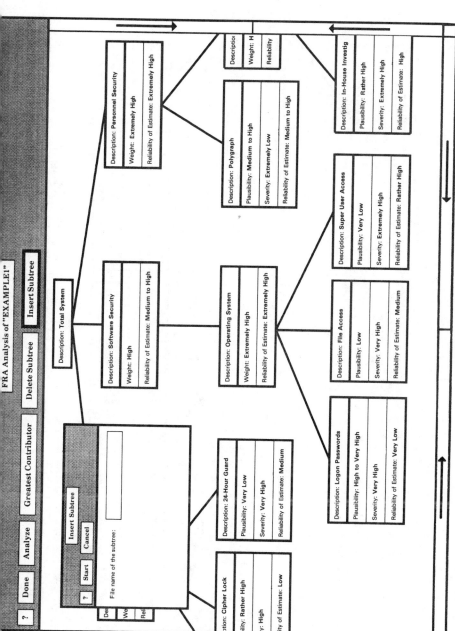

Figure 6.36 The query window generated upon invocation of the **Insert Subtree** command. Had a node *not* been selected prior to issuing this command, this window would not have been generated and the user would have received an error message to the effect that a subtree can only be inserted after a parent node is selected. In response to the generation of the query window, the user types in the name of the subtree to be inserted. This is one of the few places in this new FRA interface that typing is required.

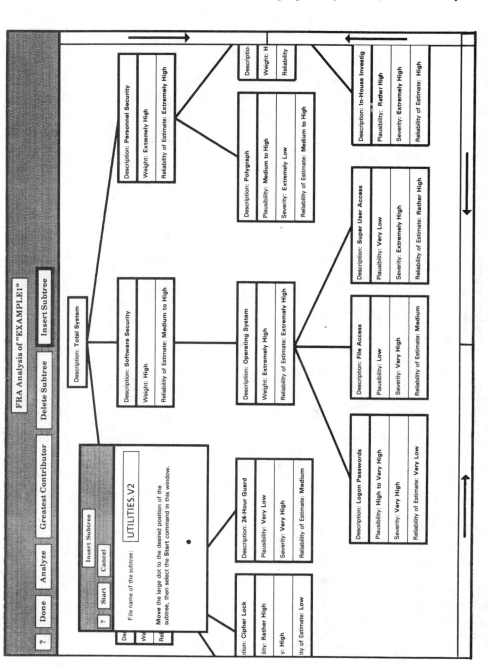

Figure 6.37 The query window now includes the request for the user to indicate the position of the new subtree by moving a

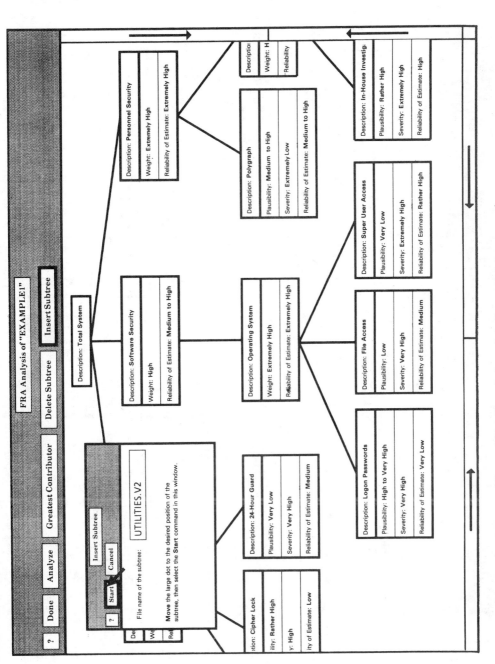

Figure 6.38 Completion of the **Insert Subtree** operation.

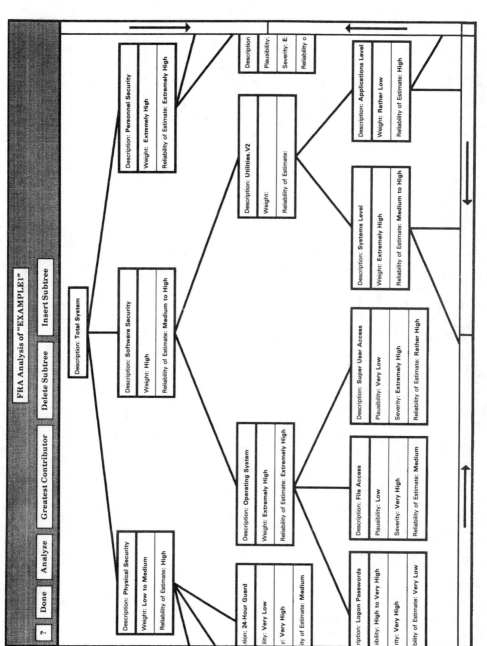

Figure 6.39 The result of the insertion of the subtree of Figure 6.32 into the tree of Figure 6.35.

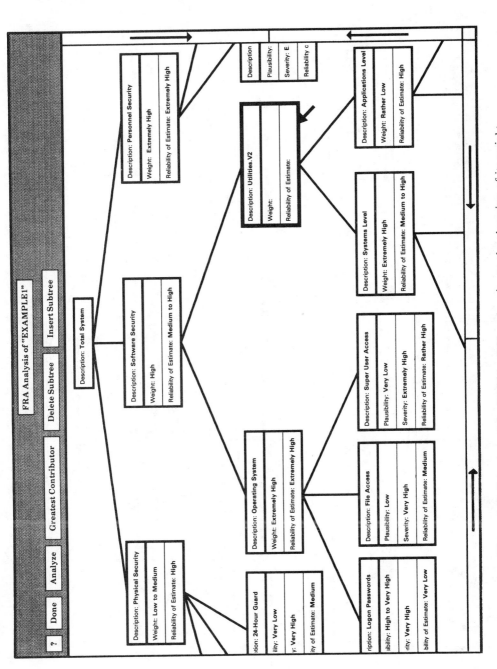

Figure 6.40 Selection of the "Utilities.V2" node prior to the changing of its weight.

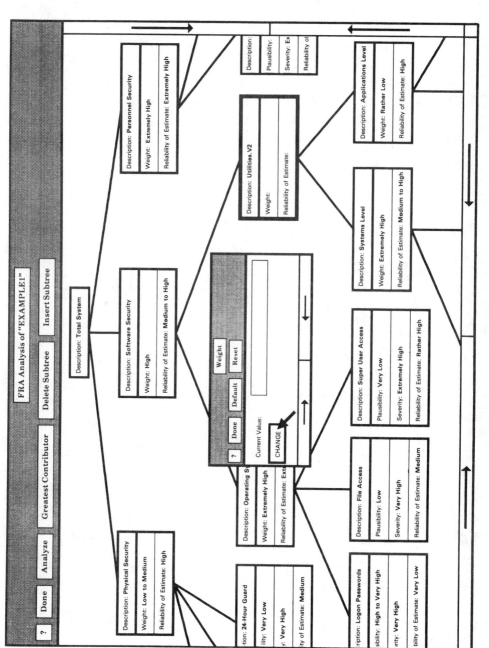

Figure 6.41 The weight property sheet displayed.

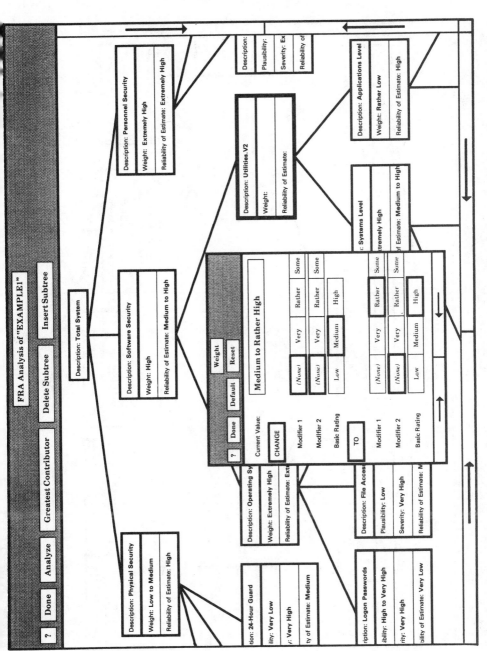

Figure 6.42 Use of the property sheet to add the weight "Medium to Rather High" to the "Utilities.V2" node. Note that this operation did not require the user to type in the new weight estimate.

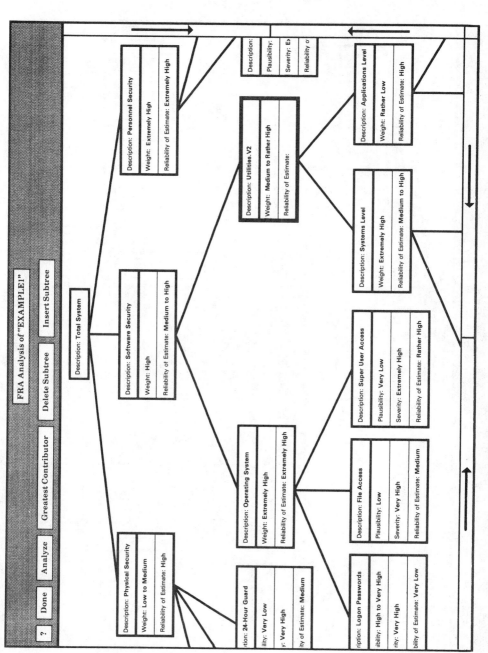

Figure 6.43 The resulting change in the weight of the "Utilities.V2" node after issuing the **Done** command in the menu portion of the weight property sheet.

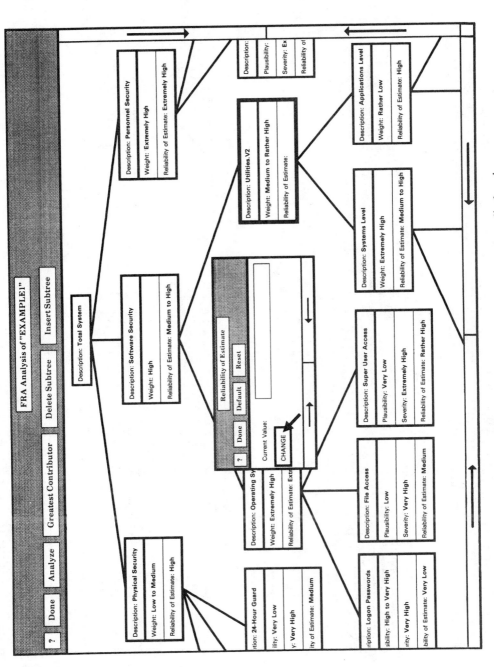

Figure 6.44 The reliability of estimate property sheet displayed.

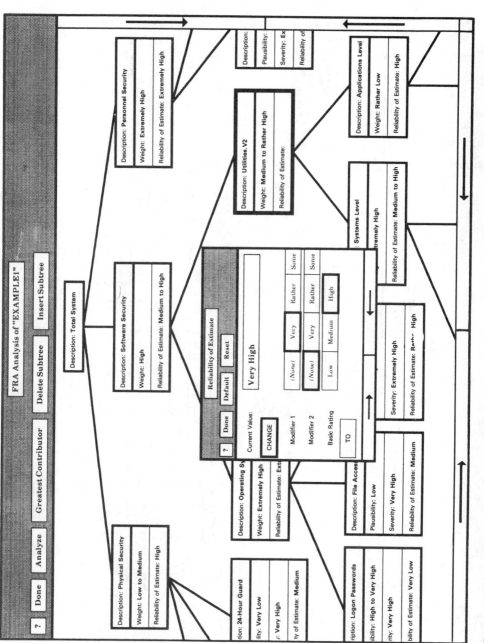

Figure 6.45 Use of the property sheet to add the reliability estimate "Very High" to the "Utilities.V2" node. Note that this operation did not require the user to type in the new estimate.

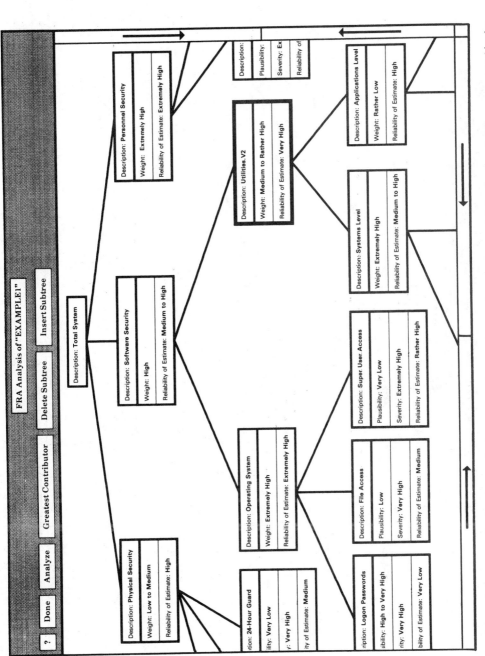

Figure 6.46 The resulting change in the reliability of estimates of the "Utilities.V2" node after issuing the **Done** command in the menu portion of the reliability of estimate property sheet.

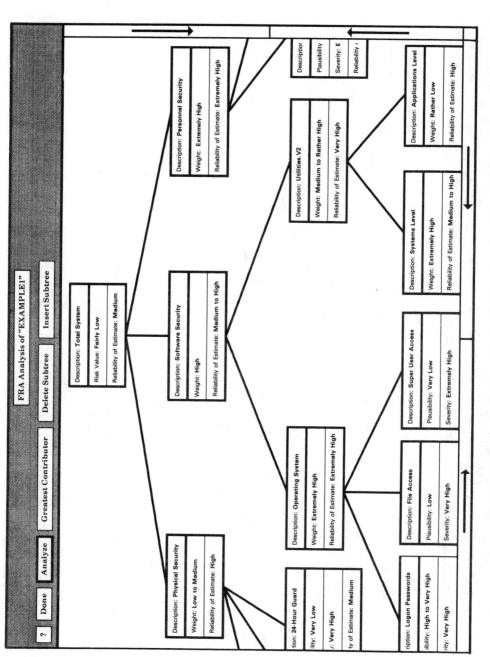

Figure 6.47 The result of the analysis of the entire tree of Figure 6.46.

We can find no better concluding remarks for this text than these of Zadeh:

In this as well as in the preceding sections, our main concern has centered on the development of a conceptual framework for what may be called a *linguistic approach* to the analysis of complex or ill-defined systems and decision processes. The substantive differences between this approach and the conventional quantitative techniques of systems analysis raise many issues and problems which are novel in nature and hence require a great deal of additional study and experimentation. This is true, in particular, of some of the basic aspects of the concept of a linguistic variable on which we have dwelt only briefly in our exposition, namely: linguistic approximation, representation of linguistic hedges, ..., and others.

Although the linguistic approach is orthogonal to what have become the prevailing attitudes in scientific research, it may well prove to be a step in the right direction, that is, in the direction of lesser preoccupation with exact quantitative analyses and greater acceptance of the pervasiveness of imprecision in much of human thinking and perception. It is our belief that, by accepting this reality rather than assuming that the opposite is the case, we are likely to make more real progress in the understanding of the behavior of humanistic systems than is possible within the confines of traditional methods [Zadeh, 1975]

Appendix A

FORMAL DEFINITION OF
A LINGUISTIC VARIABLE

A linguistic variable, X, is a 4-tuple (T, U, G, M) where

- T is the set of natural language terms which X may assume as values;
- U is the universe of discourse;
- G is a grammar (usually a context-free grammar) which generates the elements of T. $G = <V_t, V_n, P, S>$ where the V_t is the set of terminals (the primary terms and hedges of T), V_n is the set of non-terminals, P is the set of productions for generating T, and S is the start symbol. Thus, we have that $T = L(G) =$ the language generated by G; and
- M is a mapping from T to the set of fuzzy subsets of U.

Examined from another viewpoint, a linguistic variable consists of two parts: (1) a *syntactic* part which describes (a) the set of natural language expressions that are the values of the linguistic variable as well as (b) the structure of that set, and (2) a *semantic* part that associates with each natural language expression a fuzzy subset. The syntactic parts of the above formal definition are T and G; the semantic parts are M and U. While M could assign fuzzy meanings to the elements of T in any manner whatsoever, it is often useful if the meaning M assigns to a particular element of T is a function of its derivation in G. If this is the case, X is said to be a *structured* linguistic variable. All of the linguistic variables used in the main body of this text are structured. Thus, for a structured variable, X, one could algorithmically construct the meaning, $M(t)$, for a particular t in T using synthesized and inherited attributes (a la Knuth[1]) or a syntax-directed translation scheme (a la Aho and Ullman.[2] This, in fact, is done in the Fuzzy Risk Analyzer.

---

[1]Knuth, D. E., "Semantics of Context-Free Languages", *Mathematical Systems Theory*, vol. 2, no. 2, (1968), 127–145

[2]Aho, A. V., and Jeffrey D. Ullman, *Principles of Compiler Design*, Addison Wesley, (1977)

Appendix B

THE EXTENSION PRINCIPLE

The extension principle provides a mechanism to extend the domain of a given function to include fuzzy sets. Let $f: U \to V$ and let

$$A = \{a(i)/i \mid i \text{ is an element of } U\}$$

be a fuzzy subset of U. Then the definition of f can be extended to include the set of fuzzy subsets of U in the following way: Define

$$f(A) = f(\{a(i)/i \mid i \text{ is an element of U}\})$$
$$= \{a(i)/f(i) \mid i \text{ is an element of } U\}$$

Thus, the image of a fuzzy set under a mapping f is just the fuzzy set formed by mapping each of the points of the fuzzy set and associating with the mapped points the same degree of membership as their pre-images under f. This method of extending the definition of a function has analogs in probability theory (the probability distribution induced by a mapping) and in systems theory (the linear superposition principle) [Zadeh, 1975].

For functions of one variable, the extension principle appears both reasonable and intuitive. When it is applied to functions of more than one variable, however, it is considerably more complex. Consider the following case, which is representative of the types of situations most commonly observed when dealing with linguistic variables: Let $f: U_1 \times U_2 \to V$ and let A be a fuzzy subset of $U_1 \times U_2$, i.e.,

$$A = \{a(i,j)/(i,j) \mid i \in U_1, j \in U_2\}$$

Then, a straightforward application of the extension principle yields

$$f(A) = \{a(i,j)/f(i,j) \mid i \in U_1, j \in U_2\}$$

However, it is often the case that the function $a(i,j)$ is not known directly, but only through its projections on U_1 and U_2, respectively. To be able to "reconstruct" $a(i,j)$ from those projections, $a_1(i)$ and $a_2(j)$, requires that those projections be independent, in a sense similar to that when random variables are said to be independent. Zadeh has defined a fuzzy analog of independence, called *non-interaction*. Simply stated, a fuzzy subset of $U_1 \times U_2$ is non-interactive if it is separable into its two projections. Thus, to "reconstruct" such a non-interactive fuzzy set, one need only use the fuzzy cross product. The fuzzy cross product (or fuzzy Cartesian product) of two sets,

$$A = \{a(i)/i \mid i \in U_1\}$$

$$B = \{b(j)/j \mid j \in U_2\}$$

is

$$A \times B = \{\min(a(i), b(j))/(i,j) \in U_1 \times U_2\}.$$

Therefore, the definition of $f(A)$ becomes

$$f(A) = \{\min(a_1(i), a_2(j))/f(i,j) \mid i \in U_1, j \in U_2\}$$

It is this use of the extension principle, with the tacit understanding that the variables are non-interactive, that leads, for example, to the definition of the sum of two fuzzy sets:

$$
\begin{aligned}
f(A, B) = A + B &= \{\min(a(i), b(j)/f(i, j) \mid i \in A, j \in B\} \\
&= \{\min(a(i), b(j)/[i + j] \mid i \in A, j \in B\}
\end{aligned}
$$

Appendix C

IMPLEMENTATION OF FUZZY SETS

We have now shown how fuzzy sets can be a useful mathematical model for natural language estimates in an automated risk analysis utility and have even carried out a sample calculation for one particular utility, the Fuzzy Risk Analyzer. We have not yet shown how fuzzy sets can actually be implemented in a computer. We will do this now in a manner similar to our initial presentation of fuzzy set theory: as an extension/generalization of ordinary set theory.

The most "natural" computer representation of an ordinary set is as a bit-vector. In this representation scheme, any subset of, say, a 300-element universe can be represented by a 300-long binary vector. Each element of the universe is identified with an integer from 0 to 299 and a particular element of the universe is in a subset, A, if its corresponding bit is one in the binary vector corresponding to A. If an element is not present in A, its corresponding bit is set to zero. The bit corresponding to a given element, say the ith element, is the ith bit past the start of the 300-long bit vector representing the set A. This representation is a direct analog to the characteristic function of A, a concept we studied in the Introduction. This representation is a natural one if one intends to perform unions, intersections, and take the complement of the sets so represented because these operations are very naturally implemented with this set representation. To implement the set union operation, for example, one would use a bit-by-bit logical OR between the two binary vectors representing the set arguments to the union operator. If, however, the only operations to be performed are the union of disjoint sets and the determination of which member of a group of disjoint sets contains a specific element, then a binary tree representation becomes a very natural and very efficient set representation.[1] What determines whether a particular type of data representation is a natural, or an efficient choice for the implementation of a particular object is the *operations* which will be performed on that object plus the relative frequencies of those operations. We shall use the term *data structure* to describe the set of operations and their interrelations that

---

[1] Horowitz, E. and Sahni, S. *Fundamentals of Data Structures*. Computer Science Press, Rockville, Maryland, 1976, 248-257.

are to be applied to a particular object (or data object). Figure C.1 shows such a data structure for the natural numbers (taken from Horowitz and Sąhni).

What we have defined for the set of natural numbers is also called an abstract data type. Formally, an abstract data type is a triple (D, F, A) where

- D is the set of the various objects that are being operated on. In our natural number example, $D = \{natno, boolean.\}$.
- F is a set of functions defined on the objects in D. In the natural number example, $F = \{ZERO, ISZERO, SUCC, ADD\}$.
- A is a set of axioms defining the properties (that are important for the purposes at hand) of the functions and the objects. In our example, there are seven axioms that express succinctly the essential properties of the natural numbers, e.g., zero is not the successor of any natural number (ISZERO $(SUCC(x)) ::= false$); $0 + y = y$ $(ADD(ZERO(\,), y) ::= y)$; $x + 1 = y + 1 \Leftrightarrow x = y$ (EQ(SUCC(x), SUCC(y)) ::= EQ(x,y)), etc. These axioms then define all the salient properties of the objects with which we will be dealing.

An *implementation of an abstract data type* is a mapping of each of the objects of D to (usually) the primitive data types of a programming language and a

structure NATNO
   declareZERO( ) → natno
        ISZERO(natno) → boolean
        SUCC(natno) → natno
        ADD(natno, natno) → natno
        EQ(natno, natno) → boolean

   for all $x, y \in$ natno **let**

        ISZERO(ZERO( )) ::= **true**;
        ISZERO(SUCC(x)) ::= **false**
        ADD(ZERO( ),y) ::= y
        ADD(SUCC(x), y) ::= SUCC(ADD(x, y)
        EQ(x, ZERO( )) ::= **if** ISZERO(x) **then true**
                                      else false
        EQ(ZERO( ), SUCC (y)) ::= **false**
        EQ(SUCC(x), SUCC (y)) ::= = EQ (x,y)
   end
end NATNO

Figure C.1   The Abstract Data Structure "Natural Number."

mapping of each of the functions of F to programs in that language in such a way that the axioms of A are preserved. If the axioms were judiciously chosen, then no other properties are important. The implementor is only liable for upholding the specified axioms and is otherwise free to do anything in his implementation that does not cause the violation of any of the axioms. Any problems that arise because of this freedom given to the implementor are the responsibility of the data structure designer.

Now we will define an abstract data type for fuzzy sets. This is a decidedly non-trivial task, so we will approach it incrementally. First, an abstract data type for ordinary sets will be constructed and then, using the knowledge gained from this, an abstract data type for fuzzy sets will be described. Only after the fuzzy set abstract data type is completely specified will we talk of the actual implementation to realize the fuzzy sets.

Figure C.2 depicts an abstract data type for ordinary sets of natural numbers. The only objects needed are the natural numbers and the object of concern, the sets of natural numbers. A set of eight functions is also given in Figure C.2 along with 14 axioms that describe the properties of those objects and functions. Note that the names of those functions are mnemonics which (hopefully) assist the reader, but one should not infer any properties from, for example, the name 'UNION'. The properties of this particular function are only those that can be demonstrated from the 14 axioms. As an example, we see from the axiom

$$\text{UNION}(A, \text{NEW}()) ::= A$$

that the result of the UNION operation on any set A and the set returned by the constant function NEW is just the set A. This corresponds to the result from set theory that the union of any set, A, with the empty set is the set A. The axiom

$\text{ISELEMENT}(n, \text{UNION}(A, B)) ::=$
           if $\text{ISELEMENT}(n, A)$ **then true else** $\text{ISELEMENT}(n, B)$

details the properties of the ISELEMENT function with respect to the UNION function. In particular we see that the result of UNION (in so far as ISELEMENT is concerned) is a logical function of the result of the ISELEMENT function on the arguments to UNION.

Note 1 The reader unfamiliar with such an axiomatic representation of a mathematical entity should study this set example in some detail. Convince yourself that, for example, DeMorgan's Laws

$$(A \cup B)' = A' \cap B'$$

$$(A \cap B)' = A' \cup B'$$

structure SET
  declare NEW( ) → set
        UNION(set, set) → set
        INTER(set, set) → set
        COMP(set) → set
        SING(natno) → set
        ISELEMENT(natno, set) → boolean
        ISEMPTY(set) → boolean
        EQUAL(set, set) → boolean
  for all A, B ϵ set, n ϵ natno **let**
        ISEMPTY(NEW( )) ::= **true**
        ISEMPTY(SING(n)) ::= **false**
        ISEMPTY(UNION(A, SING(n))) ::= **false**
        ISEMPTY(COMP(SING(n))) ::= **false**
        UNION(A, NEW( )) ::= A
        INTER(A, NEW( )) ::= NEW( )
        INTER(SING(n), SING(m)) ::=
                if $n = m$ **then** SING(n) **else** NEW( )
        EQUAL(A, B) ::=
           if ISELEMENT(n, A) = ISELEMENT(n, B) **then true**
           else false
        ISELEMENT(n, NEW( )) ::= **false**
        ISELEMENT(n, SING(m)) ::= **if** $n = m$ **then true**
                            else false
        ISELEMENT(n, UNION(A, B)) ::=
           if ISELEMENT(n, A) **then true**
           else ISELEMENT(n, B)
        ISELEMENT(n, INTER(A, B)) :=
           if ISELEMENT(n, A) **then** ISELEMENT(n, B)
           else false
        ISELEMENT(n, COMP(A)) ::=
           if ISELEMENT(n, A) **then false**
           else true
  end
end SET

Figure C.2   An Abstract Data Structure for 'SET'

are provable from this axiom set. This would mean that DeMorgan's Laws hold in any implementation that faithfully preserves the axioms. The implementor need not concern himself with this particular result in set theory (or any of the myriad others)—just the axioms.

Note 2 The astute reader may have noticed that the axiom

$$\text{UNION}(A, \text{NEW}()) ::= A$$

is not really needed. It can be derived from the following three axioms:

ISELEMENT(n, NEW()) ::= **false**

ISELEMENT(n, UNION(A,B)) ::=
        if ISELEMENT(n, A) **then true**
        else ISELEMENT(n, B)

EQUAL(A, B) ::=
        if *ISELEMENT(n, A)* = ISELEMENT(n, B) **then true**
        else false

This is not an accident. The set of axioms was purposely not made *minimal* for pedagogical reasons. Hopefully, in including some redundant axioms for such purposes, no inconsistent one slipped by the author!

    Figure C.3 is an abstract data type for fuzzy sets over the natural numbers. In this abstract data type we have:

- $D = \{$natno, fuzset, boolean, fuzmap$\}$ where fuzmap is the set of functions mapping individual natural numbers to fuzzy subsets of the natural numbers,
- F is the set of 16 functions presented in Figure C.3.
- A is the set of 16 axioms presented in Figure C.3.

This abstract data type was modeled after the abstract data type for ordinary sets that was given in Figure C.2. Many of the functions in these two data types are identical in terms of their mapping characteristics (e.g., UNION which takes two sets (either fuzzy or ordinary) and returns a set of the same type). Other functions are different, e.g., SING which creates singleton sets. The "ordinary" SING has only one argument, a natural number; the fuzzy SING has two arguments: a natural number and a real number which will become the degree of membership. Still others are completely new, e.g., ADD, CON, NORM, ... There is a correspondence between the functions ISELEMENT for ordinary sets and DEG_OF_MEM mimicking the similarity in the characteristic functions for

structure FUZSET
  declare NEW( ) → fuzset
      SING(natno, real) → fuzset
      ISEMPTY(fuzset) → boolean
      EQUAL(fuzset, fuzset) → boolean
      UNION(fuzset, fuzset) → fuzset
      INTER(fuzset, fuzset) → fuzset
      COMP(fuzset) → fuzset
      DEG_OF_MEM(natno, fuzset) → real
      ADD(fuzset, fuzset) → fuzset
      MULT(fuzset, fuzset) → fuzset
      DIV(fuzset, fuzset) → fuzset
      NORM(fuzset) → fuzset
      INT(fuzset) → fuzset
      DIL(fuzset) → fuzset
      CON(fuzset) → fuzset
      FUZ(fuzset, fuzmap) → fuzset

for all $m, n \epsilon$ natno, $A, B \epsilon$ fuzset, $r \epsilon [0, 1], f \epsilon$ fuzmap **let**
    ISEMPTY(NEW( )) ::= **true**
    ISEMPTY(SING(n, r)) ::= **false**
    EQUAL(A, B) ::=
        if DEG_OF_MEM(n, A) = DEG_OF_MEM(n, B) **then true**
        else false
    DEG_OF_MEM(n, NEW( )) ::= 0
    DEG_OF_MEM(n, SING(m, r)) ::= **if** $n = m$ **then** r **else** 0
    DEG_OF_MEM(n, *UNION*(A, B)) ::=
                max(DEG_OF_MEM(n, A), DEG_OF_MEM(n, B))
    DEG_OF_MEM(n, INTER(A, B)) ::=
                min(DEG_OF_MEM(n, A), DEG_OF_MEM(n, B))
    DEG_OF_MEM(n, COMP(A)) ::= 1 − DEG_OF_MEM(n, A)
    DEG_OF_MEM(n, ADD(A, B)) ::=
        $\max_{i+j=n}$ {min(DEG_OF_MEM(i, A), DEG_OF_MEM(j, B))}
    *DEG*_OF_MEM(n, MULT(A, B)) ::=
        $\max_{i*j=n}$ {min(DEG_OF_MEM(i, A), DEG_OF_MEM(j, B))}
    DEG_OF_MEM(n, *DIV*(A, B)) ::=
        $\max_{i/j=n}$ {min(DEG_OF_MEM(i, A), DEG_OF_MEM(j, B))}

      Figure C.3 An Abstract Data Structure for FUZSET.
               Continued on next page.

DEG_OF_MEM(i, NORM(A)) ::= 1.0, for some $i \in$ natno
DEG_OF_MEM(n, CON(A)) ::= [DEG_OF_MEM(n, A)]^2
DEG_OF_MEM(n, DIL(A)) ::= [DEG_OF_MEM(n, A)]$^{1/2}$
DEG_OF_MEM(n, INT(A)) ::=
    if $0 \leq$ DEG_OF_MEM(n, A) ≤ 0.5
    then $2 *$ [DEG_OF_MEM(n, A)]^2
    else $1.0 - 2 *$ [1 $-$ DEG_OF_MEM(n, A)]^2
DEG_OF_MEM(n, FUZ(A, f)) ::=
    max {DEG_OF_MEM(i, A) $*$ DEG_OF_MEM(n, $f(i)$))}

  end
end FUZSET

Figure C.3   An Abstract Data Structure for FUZSET. (Continued)

ordinary sets and for fuzzy sets. The functions in Figure C.3 are representative of the operations we will be performing in the fuzzy sets in our application area: natural language computations for risk analysis. Because of this, we have no function of, say, the following form:

$$F(\text{real, fuzset}) \rightarrow \text{natno}$$

This is because in our application we have no need to ask a question like "What element of a particular fuzzy set has a .2 degree of membership?"

Given this precise description of a computer implementation of fuzzy sets, we can now begin. Directly extending the bit vector implementation of ordinary sets to the fuzzy domain would have us implement fuzzy sets as arrays of real numbers. If our universe was {1, 2, 3, 4} then the fuzzy set {.5/2, .9/4} would be represented as a four-element array F, where $F(1) = 0.0$, $F(2) = 0.5$, $F(3) = 0.0$, and $F(4) = 0.9$. Looking over the operations we wish to perform on our fuzzy sets, it is easy to see that the fuzzy union and fuzzy intersection can easily be implemented as element-by-element maximum or minimum. The fuzzy operations derived from the application of the extension principle are a different matter, however. These operations, ADD, MULT, and DIV, require the base upon which the fuzzy sets are defined both to enlarge and to shrink. For example, if two fuzzy sets defined over {1, 2, 3, 4} are added together, the resulting fuzzy set is one defined over {1, 2, 3, 4, 5, 6, 7, 8}. In most computer languages, arrays cannot have variable dimensions, so this is a complication with respect to our choice of an array implementation of fuzzy sets. Note, in some of the languages that ostensibly allow variable dimensions, e.g., PL/I, one must still declare a fixed dimension each time storage is allocated (upon, for example, entry into a PL/I block). Such entities cannot dynamically change their extents—a property we need.

It might be argued that to get around this problem of varying sizes of sets, all one would have to do is to decide on the maximum size needed and then just use this maximum size for all fuzzy sets. The elements "on the end" will just have zero degrees of membership anyway if the base set is "really" smaller than that maximum. Unfortunately, problems exist in the implementation of this maximum array idea. These implementation problems are to some extent dependent on our intended application area: automated risk analysis and in particular by the methodology of system decomposition that the FRA uses as its philosophical base. Practically speaking, suppose one were to define the primary terms (of the FRA) as fuzzy subsets of $\{1, 2, 3, 4, 5, 6, 7, 8, 9\}$ and then (somehow) determine that the set $\{n \mid 1 \leq n \leq 243\}$ was a reasonable maximum upon which to base all fuzzy sets that the FRA would construct internally. This is exactly the maximum that we would have to have had to do our hand calculation for the example in the FRA section (Figure 5.3) *if* our primary terms had been defined over $\{1, 2, 3, 4, 5, 6, 7, 8, 9\}$. This is because in that example the calculation for the fuzzy weighted mean involved, as an intermediate step, the fuzzy multiplication of three pairs of fuzzy sets. Had these sets been defined over $\{n \mid 1 \leq n \leq 9\}$, then the multiplication operations would each have resulted in a fuzzy set over $\{n \mid 1 \leq n \leq 81\}$. The fuzzy sum of three such sets would have resulted in a fuzzy set defined over $\{n \mid 1 \leq n \leq 243\}$ since $243 = 9 * 9 + 9 * 9 + 9 * 9$. (It now should be abundantly clear why the primary terms for that example were defined over $\{1, 2, 3, 4\}$!) This would mean that for most of the fuzzy sets represented by this implementation, we would be wasting over 200 words of memory. The large number of both fuzzy sets and intermediate fuzzy sets that must be maintained in any such application of a risk analysis calculation adds up to a considerable amount of unused storage. From a practical point of view, this may make the difference between being able to implement such an automated risk analysis utility on a small machine and not being able to. Even if it is still possible, it seems like such a waste.

The other objection to the use of a maximal array to solve the varying universe size problem is that no such maximum can really be determined *a priori* in our risk analysis utility. So even if you subscribe to the MIF principle (Memory Is Free—a programming axiom of younger programmers), you will have difficulty in applying that principle in this case. In order to establish such a maximum, one would have to determine the maximum number of nodes in the system decomposition that is input to the FRA and also the maximum out-degree of any node in that decomposition. Such estimates would be very difficult to make and the only reasonable method would be to limit the out-degree to, say, 10, and then to inform the end users of the FRA not to exceed this limit. If your also choose a very restrictive maximum number of nodes of 200, then the array implementation of fuzzy sets could require as much as 162K words just for the fuzzy sets alone! (This is because the out-degree limit of ten implies an array maximum of $10 * (9 * 9)$. If there are 200 such fuzzy sets, then the maximum number of words is $200 * 10 * 9 * 9 = 162K$.) And this is with these stringent limitations on the end user. These results show us that we do not need a small perturbation of our array approach (like the maximum array modification) but rather a totally different scheme.

An alternate method of implementation for fuzzy sets is to use linked lists. Each node of the linked list representing a fuzzy set will contain the natural number base (the set part), a real number between 0 and 1 (the fuzzy part), and a link to the next node. Nodes are present only for elements with non-zero degrees of membership, much in the same way that our notation convention ignores elements with a zero degree of membership. Using this method, the fuzzy set $A = \{.5/2, .9/4, .3/7\}$ from the universe $\{1, 2, 3, 4, 5, 6, 7\}$ would be represented as

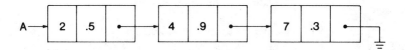

This implementation "wastes" very little storage and makes it possible to use as large a universe as necessary since the representation does not change if the universe is enlarged. If in the example given above the universe was $\{n \mid 1 \leq n \leq 200\}$ instead of $\{1, 2, 3, 4, 5, 6, 7\}$, then the representation of A would still be:

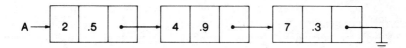

since elements with a zero degree of membership (i.e., all the elements from 8 on!) are not explicitly represented.

For ease in processing and algorithm design for the various functions that have to be programmed, we will require that the elements of any fuzzy set are in strictly increasing order with respect to the natural number component (the set part of the fuzzy set). Note that this is an implementation decision—it is part of the freedom that is (and must be) given to the system implementor. Since this decision is in the implementation domain, it is, therefore, not represented in the axioms nor does the end user need to know this in order to make use of any application program (like the FRA, for example) that employs fuzzy sets.

Given this representation for fuzzy sets, we are now faced with the problem of finding algorithms for each of the functions in the fuzzy set abstract data type in order to complete this fuzzy set implementation. An example may clarify the type of algorithm desired. The INTER function must implement the notion of a fuzzy intersection, at least in so far as it is specified by the axioms of Figure C.3. Consider the following two fuzzy sets, A and B:

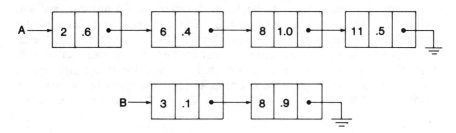

Figure C.4 Fuzzy Sets A and B.

and suppose we wish to construct the fuzzy intersection of these two sets. Since all fuzzy sets are internally ordered by the natural number component, the algorithm for taking the intersection of two fuzzy sets can make use of this property and, in addition, it *must* insure that the resulting fuzzy set conforms to this restriction. We will implement the fuzzy intersection by "stepping through" each of the lists looking for the same natural number component in each set, and if we find such an element, then this natural number will be in the fuzzy intersection. We could, of course, take each element of A and then search through the whole of B to determine if that element is present in B, but this would be extremely inefficient (or more technically, would result in a algorithm of order $\theta(mn)$ where $m = |A|$ and $n = |B|$, the cardinalities of our two sets). We can describe a much more efficient algorithm (of order $\theta(m + n)$) by taking advantage of the order property of this particular fuzzy implementation. We will do so in the following way: Two pointers, current$\_A$ and current$\_B$, will be established to "step through" the fuzzy sets A and B, starting at their respective heads. In constructing the fuzzy set $C = \text{INTER}(A, B)$, we will examine the nodes pointed to by current$\_A$ and current$\_B$. If the natural number component of the node pointed to by current$\_A$ is less than the natural number component of the node pointed to by current$\_B$, then we "step" current$\_A$ to the next node in the fuzzy set A. If it is more, then we "step" current $\_B$. If they are equal, then we have found a base element that will be in the intersection, and we construct a new node for C. The natural number component of this node will be the natural number component of the node pointed to by current$\_A$ (or the natural number component pointed to by current$\_B$, since these components are equal.) The degree of membership component of this new node in C will be the minimum of the degree of membership components of the nodes pointed to by current$\_A$ and current$\_B$. We continue in this way until either current$\_A$ or current$\_B$ becomes null (i.e., until we "fall off" the end of one of the fuzzy sets!). C then points to the intersection of A and B.

Represented as an algorithm this becomes:

```
while (there is some of A left AND some of B left) do
    begin
        if current_A → natno < current_B → natno
        then "step" current_A

        else if current_A → natno > current_B → natno
        then "step" current_B

        else       {they are equal}
        begin
            1) create new node
            2) new → natno := current_A → natno;
            3) new → degree_of_membership :=
                min (current_A → degree_of_membership,
                     current_B → degree_of_membership);

            4) link new node into C
            5) "step" both current_A and current_B
        end       {else block}
    end {while do}
```

In the example of Figure C.4, current_A starts out at the head of A and current_B at the head of B. Since $2 < 3$, current_A is moved to point to the node with natural number component 6. Since $6 > 3$, current_B is moved to the node of B with natural number component 8. Since $6 < 8$, current_A is moved to the node of A with natural number component 8. In the next repetition of the **while do** loop, a node is created with natural number component 8 and degree of membership component .9. There is no further repetition of the **while do** loop after this, since there are no additional nodes of B.

Figure C.5 presents a Pascal implementation of the algorithm given above for the intersection of two fuzzy sets. In this Pascal procedure it is assumed that the following declarations have been made elsewhere:

```
type
    fuzzypointer = ↑fuzzy;
    fuzzy =
            record
                element : integer;
                degree_of_membership : real;
                next : fuzzypointer
            end;
```

Figure C.5 Pascal Implementation of Fuzzy Intersection.
Continued on next page.

function INTER (*X, Y* : fuzzypointer) : fuzzypointer;

{This function returns the fuzzy intersection of the fuzzy sets pointed to by *X* and *Y*. The supports of *X* and *Y* need not be identical. }

    var *A, B, C*, cur*C*, temp : fuzzypointer; {current pointers}
    begin
        {Initialize all pointers and create dummy head node for *C*, the fuzzy set that will be the fuzzy intersection of *X* and *Y*. The dummy head node will simplify the coding of the remainder of this function. This dummy head node will be "skipped over" before INTER returns the fuzzy intersection.}

        new(*C*); *C*↑.next := nil; cur*C* := *C*;
        A := *X*;   *B* := *Y*;

        while ((*A* <> nil) AND (*B* <> nil)) **do**
        if *A*↑.element < *B*↑.element
          then *A* := *A*↑.next
          else if *A*↑.element > *B*↑.element
              then *B* := *B*↑.next
            else   {Equal elements}
            begin
              new(temp);   {Construct new node}
              temp↑.element := *A*↑.element;
              temp↑.degree_of_membership :=
                min(*A*↑.degree_of_membership,
                    B↑.degree_of_membership);
              temp↑.next := nil;

              cur*C*↑.next := temp;   {Link into intersection set}
              cur*C* := temp

              A := *A*↑. next ; {Go to next element of both sets.}
              B := *B*↑. next

            end;
      {end while do}
        INTER := *C*↑.next   {Delete dummy node and return}
    end;   {INTER}

Figure C.5 Pascal Implementation of Fuzzy Intersection.
(Continued)

In this Pascal implementation, we have simplified the algorithm by slightly complicating the structure of the fuzzy set *C*. In order to make the algorithm work uniformly for both the initial element of *C* and on all other elements, we have added a dummy node to *C*. The use of this dummy node insures, for the purposes of the design of the **while do** loop, that *C* has at least one node. Upon termination of the **while do** loop, we merely adjust *C* by "jumping over" the dummy node. Note that the use of such a programming technique (related to the sentinel technique detailed by Wirth[2]) in no way violates the condition that a linked list representing a fuzzy set be ordered with respect to the natural number component. We are only obliged to follow such restrictions "outside" our implementation of the functions, i.e., we must *return* only linked lists that follow this restriction.

The implementation of the UNION function is quite similar to that of the INTER function, but somewhat more complicated. As in the implementation of the INTER function, we will make use of two pointers, current_A and current_B, to step through the lists *A* and *B*. In constructing *C* = UNION(*A*, *B*), we will examine the nodes pointed to by current_A and current_B. If the natural number component of the node pointed to by current_A (suppose it is *n*) is less than the natural number component of the node pointed to by current_B, then we know that the fuzzy set *B* will make no contribution to the *n* component of *C*. This is because of the ordering restriction on the linked list representation of fuzzy sets and because of the manner of stepping current_B through the list *B* implies that *B* has no *n* component. We append to the list *C* (now being constructed) a *copy* of the node pointed to by current_A and then step current_A to the next node of *A*.

Extending these ideas for the UNION function results in the following algorithm:

```
begin
    while (there is some of A left AND some of B left) do
        begin
            if current_A → natno < current_B → natno
            then begin
                1) copy A's current node and append to the end of C
                2) "step" current_A
            end
            else if current_A → natno > current_B → natno
            then begin
                1) copy B's current node and append to the end of C
                2) "step" current_B
            end
```

[2]Wirth, Nicklaus, *Algorithms + Data Structures = Programs*, Englewood Cliffs, NJ: Prentice-Hall. 1976.

           else {they are equal}
      begin
          1) Construct a new node for C using natno from A's current node
              and the MAX of the degree of membership from A's current
              node and B's current node.
          2) "step" both current_A and current_B
      end
    end   {while do}

Append leftover portion of A or B (whichever is left) to the end of C

  end

    Figure C.6 presents a Pascal implementation of the algorithm given above for the union of two fuzzy sets. This implementation also makes use of the sentinel technique used in the implementation of the fuzzy intersection. In addition, this Pascal procedure for the fuzzy union makes use of the technique of functional decomposition in the use of two procedures which, respectively, copy one node of a linked list, and copy the remaining portion of a linked list. The use of such procedures simplifies the total UNION procedure and makes its comprehension by others (unfortunately, an oft-forgotten objective) considerably easier.
    Since it is not our goals here to present an implementation of every one of the functions in our FUZSET data structure, we shall not describe implementations of NEW, SING, ISEMPTY, EQUAL, COMP, or DEG_OF_MEM. They represent relatively straightforward extensions of the techniques we have detailed for INTER and UNION. Of the remaining functions, those derived from an applica-

```
function UNION (X, Y : fuzzypointer) : fuzzypointer;
  var A, B, C, curC : fuzzypointer;        {Current pointers}
  procedure copy_at_end (    node_to_be_inserted : fuzzypointer;
                        var current_end_node : fuzzypointer);
    {Make a copy of the node pointed to by node_to_be_inserted and append
    this new node to the node pointed to by current_end_node. Note: it is
    assumed that there is no node after current_end_node. i.e., it is assumed
    that current_end_node is the end of a list. After this procedure terminates,
    current_end_node still points to the end of a list—a list that is exactly one
    node longer than it was before this procedure was invoked.}
  begin
      new(current_end_node↑.next);
      current_end_node := current_end_node↑.next;
      current_end_node↑ := node_to_be_inserted↑;
      current_end_node↑.next := nil
  end;        {copy_at_end}
```

Figure C.6 Pascal Implementation of the Fuzzy Union.
Continued on next page.

```
procedure copyall_at_end (    first_node_to_be_inserted : fuzzypointer;
                         var current_end_node : fuzzypointer);
    {Make a copy of the node pointed to by first_node_to_be_inserted and
    all following nodes and append them to the node pointed to by cur-
    rent_end_node. Note that current_end_node points to the end of a list.
    After this procedure terminates, current_end_node still points to the end
    of a list.}
begin
    while (first_node_to_be_inserted <> nil) do
        begin
            copy_at_end(first_node_to_be_inserted, current_end_node);
            first_node_to_be_inserted := first_node_to_be_inserted↑.next
        end
end;        {copyall_at_end}


begin    {Main body of UNION}
    {Create dummy node for C and establish temporary pointers to the head of the
    fuzzy sets of which the union is being constructed.}

    new(C); C↑.next := nil; curC := C;
    A := X;     B := Y;

    {Perform main part of set union}
    while ((A <> nil) AND (B <> nil)) do
        if A↑.element < B↑.element
            then begin
                    copy_at_end(A, curC);
                    A := A↑.next
                end
        else if A↑.element > B↑.element
                then begin
                        copy_at_end(B, curC);
                        B := B↑.next
                    end
                else    {Equal elements}
                begin
                    copy_at_end(A, curC);    {Get MOST of new current node}
                    curC↑.degree_of_membership :=
                    max(A↑.degree_of_membership,
                        B↑.degree_of_membership);
                    A := A↑.next;
                    B := B↑.next
                end
    {end while do}
```

Figure C.6 Pascal Implementation of the Fuzzy Union.
Continued on next page.

{At this point, all of either A or B (or both!) is in the union, i.e., A or B (or both) are nil. Add the remaining elements to the union, then remove the dummy node from C before returning to the calling program.}

```
if A <> nil
  then copyall_at_end(A, curC)
  else      {A = nil}
  if B <> nil
    then copyall_at_end(B, curC);

UNION := C↑.next

end;    {UNION}
```

Figure C.6 Pascal Implementation of the Fuzzy Union. (Continued)

tion of the extension principle (ADD, MULT, and DIV) present some new difficulties, and thus provide an additional pedagogical opportunity. Accordingly, we shall detail an implementation of MULT.

The implementation of the MULT function will take full advantage of the flexibility of our linked list representation for fuzzy sets, i.e., the ability to insert new elements at any point easily and efficiently, and the ability to grow and shrink the set size dynamically at execution time. Basically, our implementation of MULT is as follows: for each node in the list A, we will step through the nodes of the list B, and for each node of B, we will (potentially) construct a new node for the list $C = \text{MULT}(A, B)$—a node that will be inserted in the list C in its proper position.

Represented as an algorithm this becomes:

```
while (there is some of A left) do
  begin
    current_B := B;
    while (there is some of B left) do
      begin
        1) construct values for new node based on values of nodes pointed
           to by current_A and current_B
        2) insert new node into C
        3) "step" current_B
      end {while for the list B}
    "step" current_A
  end     {while for the list A}
```

Figure C.7 presents a Pascal implementation of the algorithm given above for the multiplication of two fuzzy sets. As before, we have made use of additional

function MULT (*X, Y* : fuzzypointer) : fuzzypointer;
  var *A, B, C*, cur*C*, ptr, beforeptr : fuzzypointer;
    base : integer;
    degreeofmembership : real;
  procedure insert(natno : integer;
                membership : real;
                  X : fuzzypointer);
{Assume that *X* has at least two nodes, one with the minimum possible natural number component and one with the maximum. Insert a new node with 'natno' as the element and 'membership' as the degree_of_membership at the appropriate position. Recall that the link list representation for fuzzy sets used here requires that the nodes be in increasing order of the element field. Also, note that this assumes univalent nodes, i.e., there is only one pointer to each node. }
    var done : boolean;   {'done' will be set to true when the insertion is
                            complete}
    current_node, temp_node : fuzzypointer;
  begin   {Body of insert}
    done := false;
    current_node := *X*;
    while ((current_node <> nil) AND (NOT done)) **do**
      begin
        if current_node↑.element = natno
          then begin   {same base found—fix up degree of membership only}
              current_node↑.degree_of_membership :=
                  max(current_node↑.degree_of_membership,
                      membership);
              done := true
          end

        else if current_node↑.element > natno
          then begin   {Insert new node BEFORE the node pointed
                        to by current_node}
              new(temp_node);
              temp_node↑ := current_node;
              current_node↑.element := natno;
              current_node↑.degree_of_membership :=
              membership;
              current_node↑.next := temp_node;
              done := true
          end;

Figure C.7 Pascal Implementation of Fuzzy Multiplication.
Continued on next page.

```
            current_node := current_node↑.next;
      end      {while do}
   end;      {insert}

begin      {Main body of MULT}
{Prepare dummy nodes for the list C}
new(C);   C↑.element := 0;              {First node}
new(C↑.next)  C↑.next .element := maxint; C↑.next↑.next := nil; {Last node}
A := X;     B := Y;

{Main body of the multiplication function}
while(A <> nil) do
   begin
      B := Y;
      while (B <> nil) do
         begin   {Construct new node for the list C}
            base := A↑.element * B↑.element;
            degreeofmembership :=
                  min(A↑.degree_of_membership,
                        B↑.degree_of_membership);
            insert(base, degreeofmembership, C);

            B = B↑.next
         end;      {while for the B list}

      A := A↑.next
   end;      {while for the A list}

{Fix up the list C before returning it by deleting the last node (the node with
 element value maxint.)}
ptr := C↑.next;   beforeptr := C;
while (ptr ↑.next <> nil) do
   begin
      ptr := ptr↑.next;
      beforeptr := beforeptr↑.next
   end;

beforeptr↑.next := nil;      {Remove last node}

MULT := C↑.next      {Remove first node and return}

end;      {MULT}
```

Figure C.7   Pascal Implementation of Fuzzy Multiplication. (Continued)

programming "tricks" to simplify the Pascal code. The most significant of these is in the initialization of the list C. This list is initialized to have the following value:

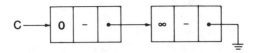

This is done to simplify the insert procedure. With this initial value, the insert procedure just has to search for the first node of C whose element component either equals or exceeds the element component of the node to be inserted *and* it is guaranteed that one of these will occur! If a node is found in the list C with element component equal to the element component to be inserted, then the degree of membership of this node is (potentially) adjusted. If an element component with a value greater than that of the node to be inserted is found, then the new node is inserted *before* the node with the higher element value. The insertion of a new node before a given node is usually thought to be a difficult if not impossible operation in a singly linked list, such as we have here representing fuzzy sets. Wirth presents a truly clever method to accomplish this task.[3] Suppose the situation is as sketched below and one wishes to insert the node pointed to by q before a particular node in a list—the node pointed to by p:

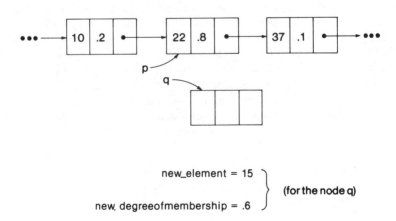

new_element = 15   ⎤
                   ⎬ (for the node q)
new degreeofmembership = .6   ⎦

Figure C.8A   Node Insertion.

[3]Wirth, Nicklaus, *Algorithms + Data Structures = Programs*, Englewood Cliffs, NJ: Prentice-Hall, (1976) 172.

One just inserts q *after* p and then switches the values for the element and the degree of membership components, using, for example, the following Pascal code:

```
q↑ := p↑; {Stores 22 and .8 in the q node, as well
                as the link to p's successor}
p↑.element := new_element;
p↑.degreeofmembership := new_degreeofmembership;
p↑.next := q;
```

This situation then becomes:

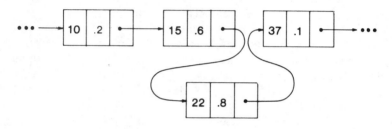

Figure C.8B   Node Insertion.

which is precisely what is desired! The only difficulty with this algorithm for the inclusion of a node before a given node in a singly linked list is that it implicitly assumes that no other pointer points to the given node. If it happened, in our example above, that some other entity pointed to the node p, then this technique would incorrectly disturb that pointer's referent. All of the nodes in our implementation of fuzzy sets are *univalent*, however, i.e., they are pointed to by, at most, one pointer. It is not the case that if two fuzzy sets both happened to contain the element 12 with degree of membership .032, that the node with these values would be *shared* between these fuzzy sets. Each would contain a separate copy of the node and, thus, the Wirth technique is appropriate.

ANNOTATED BIBLIOGRAPHY

This annotated bibliography represents the results of an extensive review of the literature regarding the use of fuzzy set theory for the modeling of natural language expressions, especially with respect to the fields of computer security and risk analysis. While this bibliography does include a large number of papers on a variety of topics related to fuzzy sets, no attempt was made to include *every* paper in the immense literature of fuzzy sets. (For such a comprehensive review see [Gaines and Kohout, 1977] and [Gupta, 1979].) Rather, this bibliography concentrates on those papers that would be immediately useful to the person interested in pursuing the topics addressed in this short book and whose primary background in fuzzy sets and their applications is just the material presented here. The annotations in this bibliography should assist the reader in determining whether or not the original article is relevant to his particular needs. In a few cases, citations were found for papers which appeared to be relevant to the goal of this text but which were not read during its preparation because they were in proceedings or journals not easily obtained or because of the time constraints imposed on its production. These citations appear in the bibliography so as not to lose these pointers into the literature — pointers to papers and research efforts which may be relevant to the reader's needs. These unread works may be identified in the bibliography which follows either by the absence of any annotation following the reference or by the words "(Bibliographic Abstract only)" following the abstract of the reference obtained from a bibliographic service.

To assist the reader who wishes to use this bibliography directly, the bibliographic entries have been cross-referenced by the following subject headings:

- Applications of Fuzzy Set Theory

- Computer Implementations of Fuzzy Sets

- Computer Security

- Fuzzy Logic and Fuzzy Reasoning

- Fuzzy Set Theory

- Linguistic Applications of Fuzzy Set Theory

- Psychological Aspects of Fuzziness

- Risk Analysis

Applications of Fuzzy Set Theory

[Adamo, 1980] [Addanki, 1979], [Bellman and Lee, 1978], [Braae and Rutherford, 1979], [Chaudhuri *et al*., 1980], [Clements, 1977], [Czogala and Pedrycz, 1981], [Dubois and Prade, 1979A], [Feagans and Biller, 1978], [Franksen, 1979], [Freeling, 1980], [Gaines and Kohout, 1977], [Goguen, 1974], [Gupta, Ragade, and Yager, 1979], [Gupta, Saridis, and Gaines, 1977], [Hoffman, Michelman, and Clements, 1978], [Hoffman and Neitzel, 1980], [Jain *et al*., 1980], [Johannsen and Rouse, 1979], [Kandel, 1978], [Kaufmann, 1977], [Koksalan and Dagli, 1981], [Lientz, 1977], [Mamdani and Gaines, 1981], [Milling, 1980], [Nguyen, 1977], [Okuda, 1978], [Papis and Mamdani, 1977], [Procyk and Mamdani, 1979], [Rine, 1979], [Rouse, 1979], [Rouse, 1980], [Tribus, 1980], [Watson *et al*., 1979], [Wenstop, 1976], [Wenstop, 1979], [Yager, 1978B], [Yao, 1979], [Yezhkova and Pospelov, 1977], [Zadeh, Fu, Tanaka, and Shimura, 1975], [Zadeh, 1976], [Zimmermann, 1979]

Computer Implementations of Fuzzy Sets

[Adamo, 1980], [Baldwin and Guild, 1979], [Clements, 1977], [Dodds, 1981], [Giles, 1980], [Hoffman, Michelman, and Clements, 1978], [Kickert, 1979], [Koppelaar and Van Der Linden, 1980], [Milling, 1980], [Shaket, 1975], [Wenstop, 1976] [Wenstop, 1979], [Zadeh, 1977A], [Zadeh, 1978]

Computer Security

[Beeler, 1979], [Clements, 1977], [Hoffman, Michelman, and Clements, 1978], [Nagy and Hoffman, 1981], [Rine, 1979]

Fuzzy Logic and Fuzzy Reasoning

[Baldwin, 1979A], [Baldwin, 1979B], [Baldwin and Pilsworth, 1979A], [Czogala and Pedrycz, 1981], [Fox, 1981], [Gaines, 1977], [Giles, 1979], [Goguen, 1979], [Haack, 1979], [Kaufmann, 1977], [Mamdani and Gaines, 1981], [Oden, 1979], [Robertson, 1978], [Schefe, 1980]

Fuzzy Set Theory

[Bellman and Giertz, 1973], [Baldwin and Guild, 1979A], [Dubois and Prade, 1979A], [Dubois and Prade, 1979B], [Dubois and Prade, 1980], [Jain *et al*., 1980], [Gaines, 1977], [Gaines and Kohout, 1977], [Gupta, 1977], [Gupta, Ragade, and Yager, 1979],

[Gupta, Saridis, and Gaines, 1977], [Kaufmann, 1975], [Mizumoto, 1980], [Mizumoto and Tanaka, 1979], [Nguyen, 1977], [Robertson, 1978], [Schefe, 1980], [Yager, 1978C], [Yager, 1979], [Zadeh, 1972B], [Zadeh, Fu, Tanaka, and Shimura, 1975], [Zadeh, 1977B], [Zadeh, 1979], [Zadeh, 1980], [Zimmermann, 1979]

Linguistic Applications of Fuzzy Set Theory

[Adamo, 1980], [Baldwin and Pilsworth, 1979b], [Bellman and Lee, 1978], [Bonissone, 1979], [Braae and Rutherford, 1979], [Clements, 1977], [Dodds, 1980] [Efstathiou and Tong, 1980], [Eshragh and Mamdani, 1979], [Heider, 1971], [Hersh and Caramazza, 1976], [Kickert, 1979], [Kochen, 1974], [Lakoff, 1973], [Macvicar-Whelen, 1978], [Nagy and Hoffman, 1981], [Nguyen, 1979], [Oden, 1979], [Procyk and Mamdani, 1979], [Shaket, 1975], [Tong, 1980], [Wenstop, 1976], [Wenstop, 1979], [Yager, 1978A], [Yager, 1978B], [Yager, 1980], [Yezhkova and Pospelov, 1977], [Zadeh, 1971], [Zadeh, 1972A], [Zadeh, 1975], [Zadeh, 1978], [Zadeh, 1981A], [Zadeh, 1981B]

Psychological Aspects of Fuzziness

[Brownwell and Caramazza, 1978], [Dubois and Prade, 1979B], [Fischoff, 1979], [Franksen, 1979], [Heider, 1971], [Hersh and Caramazza, 1976], [Hersh, Caramazza, and Brownwell, 1979], [Kaufmann, 1977], [Kochen, 1975], [Macvicar-Whelen, 1978], [McCloskey and Glucksberg, 1978], [Nagy and Hoffman, 1981], [Oden, 1977], [Oden, 1979], [Rubin, 1979], [Schefe, 1980], [Sticha, Weiss, and Donnell, 1979], [Yezhkova and Pospelov, 1977]

Risk Analysis

[Adamo, 1980], [Clements, 1977], [Feagans and Biller, 1978], [Fischoff, 1979], [Hoffman and Neitzel, 1980], [Information Policy, Inc., 1981], [Meadows, 1981], [Nagy and Hoffman, 1981], [U.S. Department of Commerce, 1979], [Watson, 1979]

Adamo, J.M. Fuzzy Decision Trees. *Fuzzy Sets and Systems*, vol. 4, no. 3, (1980) 207-219.

The decision trees method is extended to the case when the involved data (probabilities, cost, profits, losses) appear as words belonging to the common language whose semantic representations are fuzzy sets. First, the reason why such an extension is to be aimed at are discussed. Then, in the fuzzy case, a reformalization of the basic concepts of probability and utility theory is carried out. Finally, it is shown how these reformalized concepts can be applied to fuzzy decision trees. (Bibliographic Abstract only)

————L.P.L. - A Fuzzy Programming Language. *Fuzzy Sets and Systems*, vol. 3 no. 2, (1980), 151-179.

The L.P.L. language (Linguistic-oriented Programming Language) is a new language aiming at an implementation of the concepts of fuzzy set theory. After an introduction to the basic concepts, Adamo describes the syntactic aspects of L.P.L., i.e., the data declarations structure, the statements structure, and the general structure of L.P.L. models. (Bibliographic Abstracts only)

Addanki, S. Fuzzy Simulation Model for a Socio-Economic System. *Proceedings of the 1979 Summer Computer Simulation Conference*, Toronto, (16-18 July 1979), 377-384.

Modeling socio-economic systems requires the inference of structural relationships from economic theory, human understanding of the system, and vast amounts of data which are not directly useful. In all but the most simplistic idealization, most of human knowledge and understanding of these complex systems is intuitive. The present approaches to modeling socio-economic systems reduce this rather amorphous body of understanding to definitive or stochastic functional or differential forms, in the process destroying a large part of that body of intuitive knowledge. It is claimed that the theory of Fuzzy Algorithms provides a more suitable framework for the transformation of human understanding into models which may be implemented on a computer. The application of fuzzy set theory to simulation and the fuzzy simulation methodology are presented, and their characteristics are discussed. The approach is tested on the model of the Indian food sector, and a description of the model is presented, along with the results obtained. Trials confirm the usefulness of the model. (Bibliographic Abstract only)

Baldwin, J.F. Fuzzy Logic and Approximate Reasoning for Mixed Input Arguments. *International Journal of Man-Machine Studies*, vol. 11, (1979A), 381-396.

————Fuzzy Logic and Fuzzy Reasoning *International Journal of Man-Machine Studies*, vol. 11, (1979B), 465-480. (Reprinted in [Mamdani and Gaines, 1981])

In this paper Baldwin outlines a general approach to fuzzy logic, i.e., to systems of logic in which the truth values are not restricted to just *true* and *false* but can be represented by such terms as *very true, fairly false, almost fairly true*, etc. Baldwin claims that his approach is a generalization of infinite valued logics and that by using such a fuzzy logic and its associated fuzzy reasoning and fuzzy automata

A more sophisticated form of "world modeling" could be evolved, being able to deal with both precise and vague concepts and information, giving rise to simulations that might be more useful for the control of industrial and economic development than present-day attempts.

————and Guild, N.C.F. "On the Satisfaction of a Fuzzy Relation by a Set of Inputs," *International Journal of Man-Machine Studies*, vol. 11, (1979A), 397–404.

————and ————. FUZLOG: A Computer Program for Fuzzy Reasoning. *Proceedings of the Ninth International Symposium on Multiple-Valued Logic*, Bath, England, 29–31 May 1979, Published by the IEEE, (1979B), 37–45.

This paper is a first report on the development of a computer program for fuzzy logic reasoning. A description and listing of the program is given and a simple example computed. Fuzzy logic can be used to model complex systems in an economical manner and, hence, has wide application. The program provides a tool for the rapid realization of these models. (Bibliographic Abstract only)

————and Pilsworth, B.W. A Mode of Fuzzy Reasoning through Multi-Valued Logic and Set Theory, *International Journal of Man-Machine Studies*, vol. 11, (1979A), 351–380

————and ————, Fuzzy Truth Definition of Possibility Measure for Decision Classification. *International Journal of Man-Machine Studies*, vol. 11, (1979B), 447–463.

Beeler, J. Computer Security Breaches Viewed Difficult to Assess. *Computerworld*, vol. 13, no. 28, (July 1979), 16.

Various attempts have been made to assess the risk of computer room security breaches, but few if any of those efforts have ever succeeded, according to SRI International, Inc. consultant Norman R. Nielson. Speaking at a recent conference about risk assessment techniques, Nielson attributed the failure of most security breach studies to two causes: (1) the inability of most managers to gauge accurately the likelihood that a given type of violation will occur, and (2) the difficulty of measuring quantitatively the damage from certain kinds of security invasions. (Bibliographic Abstract only)

Bellman, R. and Giertz, M. On the Analytic Formalism of the Theory of Fuzzy Sets *Information Sciences*, vol. 5, (1973), 149–156.

Bellman and Giertz provide a proof that the only reasonable and natural way of extending the notions of set union and intersection to fuzzy sets is to use the arithmetic functions of *min* and *max* applied to the membership functions of the fuzzy sets. This is done by stating the properties that the membership function of, say, the union of two fuzzy sets must (naturally and intuitively) have with respect to the membership functions of the individual fuzzy sets. Among others, these properties include symmetry (i.e., the union of fuzzy sets A and B should be identical to the union of the fuzzy sets B and A), completeness (i.e., the union of the universe, U, with itself should be the universe), and requirements for some non-decreasing properties (e..g., if $A1$ is a fuzzy subset of a fuzzy set A, and if $B1$ is a fuzzy subset of a fuzzy set B, then the fuzzy union of $A1$ and $B1$ should be a fuzzy subset of the fuzzy union of A and B). Bellman and

Giertz proved that if these properties are desired, then the only possible definition of
the union of two fuzzy sets is the set defined by MAX of the membership functions of
the two individual sets. The benign nature of the assumed properties forms the basis for
stating that under reasonable and natural assumptions, their result holds.

It is interesting to note that a similar proof for the naturalness of the definition of the
complement of a fuzzy subset failed. Only with the introduction of an unnatural and
highly restrictive assumption were Bellman and Giertz able to show that Zadeh's
definition of the complement was uniquely determined. This result notwithstanding,
they state that

> Still, (Zadeh's definition of the complement) appears quite reasonable in
> practical applications.

Bellman and Giertz are also to be especially commended for their extremely lucid
and well written account of their work.

———— and Lee, E.S. *Decision Making, Fuzzy Set Theory, and Computers*,
NTIS Research Report (Final), 14 August 1978.

The accomplishments of a three-year research project are summarized in this report.
The project has produced a book which contains chapters on the following topics: can
computers think, decision making, puzzles, uncertainty, simulation, learning, con-
sciousness, humor, local logics, mathematical models of the mind, and communication
and ambiguity. The summary also discusses fuzzy set theory in health delivery systems
and in computers and linguistics. (Bibliographic Abstract only)

Bonissone, P.P. A Pattern Recognition Approach to the Problem of Linguistic Approximation in Systems Analysis, *Proceedings of the International Conference on Cybernetics and Society*, Denver, CO., 8-10 October 1979, Published by the IEEE, (1979),
793-798.

The problem of the linguistic approximation is defined on the basis of semantic
equivalence. The process consists of interpreting the meaning of any given membership
distribution and attaching to it a linguistic label belonging to a term set. A new
approach to the problem, based on feature selection and pattern recognition, is
introduced. Four weakly correlated features are precalculated for the distribution of
each element of the term set. The first step consists, of prescreening the term set. This is
done by evaluating the four features of the unlabelled fuzzy set and by using a weighted
Euclidean distance in the feature space. In the second step, a Bhattacharyya distance
between the distribution of the unlabeled fuzzy set and the distribution of each of these
preselected labels is determined. Then the label of the closest fuzzy set is assigned to the
unlabelled one. Some illustrative applications are shown. (Bibliographic Abstract
only)

Braae, M. and Rutherford, D.A. Theoretical and Linguistic Aspects of the Fuzzy Logic
Controller, *Automatica,* vol. 15, 5, (September 1979), 553-578.

Successful applications of the fuzzy logic controller by various researchers to a
variety of ill-defined processes motivated this theoretical study of the fuzzy logic

controller. Initially, the controller is analyzed by traditional (nonlinear) algebraic methods which are particularly useful in stability studies, provided the process is algebraically modeled. Despite the success of this technique, it suffers from a major limitation in that the algebraic model of the controller cannot directly deal with the linguistic aspects of the fuzzy logic controller. This observation leads to the introduction of a more concise, and hence more powerful, notation for representing the linguistic rules that describe the fuzzy logic controller. The so called linguistic models that arise from this notation are shown to be extremely useful for modeling highly nonlinear low-order systems and for determining, explicitly, the rules of 'optimal' fuzzy logic controllers. (Bibliographic Abstract only)

Brownell, H. and Caramazza, A Categorizing with Overlapping Categories *Memory and Cognition,* vol 6, no. 5, (1978), 481-490.

This paper describes a series of experiments to determine how people categorize when the categories are overlaping, e.g., 'high' and 'very high'. One of the major results is that the strict set-subset relationship was not always observed. There were some cases where, for example, membership in the category 'very high' did not guarantee membership is the category 'high'. Work of this type is most important to the natural modeling of such expressions in decision aids such as the Fuzzy Risk Analyzer described in the body of this text.

Bruce, A. Risk Management Information Through the Computer, *Foresight,* vol. 3, no. 11, (May 1978), 16-23.

Chaudhuri, E.B. and Majumer, D.D. Fuzzy Sets and Possibility Theory in Reliability Studies of Man-Machine Systems, *Fuzzy sets—Theory and Applications to Policy Analysis and Information Systems—Proceedings of the Symposium on Policy Analysis and Information Systems,* P.P.Wang and S.K. Chang (Eds.), Durham, North Carolina, 28-30 June 1980, 267-273. New York: Plenum-Publ, Corp. (1980).

In man-machine control and communication systems, the theory of probability alone is unsuitable for the evaluation of system reliability. The present paper introduces the theory of fuzzy sets and possibility theory for such analysis. The analysis is useful in speech recognition, medical diagnosis, and picture analysis problems. (Bibliographic Abstract only)

Clements, D. P. *Fuzzy Ratings for Computer Security Evaluation,* Ph.D. Dissertation, University of California at Berkeley, 1977.

In this dissertation, Clements proposes a new method for the evaluation of computer security systems. The central idea is the application of natural language as the vehicle for the expression of imprecise and sometimes subjective evaluations by a 'security rater' in the absence of objective measures of security performance. Clements suggests that linguistic rather than numeric measurement tools are more appropriate in this environment as his method "recognizes the imprecision and subjectivity (inherent in the evaluation of the security of computer systems) but demands a degree of consistency and exhaustiveness which doesn't exist now." The APL implementation of Clement's system is included as an appendix to the dissertation. (Note: [Wenstop, 1976] presents very similar ideas (and similar implementation of those ideas!) in a different application area than Clements.)

Czogala, E. and Pedrycz, W. Some Problems Concerning the Construction of Algorithms of Decision-Making in Fuzzy Systems, *International Journal of Man-Machine Studies*, vol. 15, (1981), 201–211.

Dodds, D.R. Fuzzy Logic Computer Implementation of Methaphor from Ordinary Language, AAAS Annual Meeting, Poster Session, (3-8 January 1981), Toronto.

Dubois, D.J. and Prade H. Operations in a Fuzzy-Valued Logic, *Information and Control*, vol. 43, no. 2, (November 1979A), 224-240.

A logical calculus is developed with propositions taking their truth values in the set of fuzzy subsets of [0, 1]. This fuzzy-valued logic is an extention of already known multivalent logics, and the associated set theory is shown to be that of fuzzy sets of type 2 on a given universe. Various interpretive functions are given for the usual connective of propositional calculus, using extended 'max' and 'min' operators. Examples of inference are provided and a compositional rule for fuzzy-valued fuzzy relations is suggested. (Bibliographic Abstract only)

————and————Various Kinds of Interactive Addition of Fuzzy Numbers—Application to Decision Analysis in Presence of Linguistic Probabilities, *Proceedings of the 18th IEEE Conference on Decision and Control,* 12-14 December 1979, Published by the IEEE, (1979B), 783-787.

After a brief recall of possibility theory and of the concept of interactivity, new results concerning different kinds of addition of fuzzy numbers are given. (To introduce these new additions, no reference to the extension principle is needed.) As an illustration, the application of one of these results to a problem (which was unsolved until now) of decision-making in the presence of linguistic probabilities is presented. (Bibliographic Abstract only).

———— and ———— *Fuzzy Sets and Systems: Theory and Applications*, New York, Academic Press, 1980.

————, and ————New Results about Properties and Semantics of Fuzzy Set— Theoretic Operators, *Fuzzy Sets — Theory and Applications to Policy Analysis and Information Systems—Proceedings of the Symposium on Policy Analysis and Information Systems,* Durham, NC, 28-30 June 1980, New York: Plenum, Press, (1980), 59-75.

In this paper, Dubois and Prade examine the different definitions that have been proposed for fuzzy operations, e.g., the fuzzy union. They outline a general approach to fuzzy set-theoretic operators and discuss some properties of subclasses of such fuzzy set-theoretic operators. A number of specific examples are given. An attempt to discuss a possible interpretation of these operators is proposed. The choice of a good operator in a given practical situation can be crucial in decision analysis, information retrieval, and pattern recognition for the purpose of aggregating several pieces of information.

Efstathiou, J. and Tong, R. M. Ranking Fuzzy Sets using Linguistic Preference Relations, *Proceedings of the Tenth International Symposium on Multi-Valued Logic* 3-5 June 1980, Published by the IEEE, (1980).

A report is presented on some preliminary results with a new approach to the problem of ranking fuzzy sets. The authors argue that previous methods are inadequate since they rely on numerical representations of the essential features of the problem and, therefore, defuzzify it. The authors prefer a linguistic representation and show how traditional concepts such as transitivity and ordering may be modified and used in this way. (Bibliographic Abstract only)

Ellison, J.R. and Waring, L.P. Computer Security: Managing the Risks, *Foresight,* vol. 3, no. 12, (June 1978), 13-23.

Although the identification and assessment of the relevant factors will depend on each organzation, five steps are essential to formulating a security policy and program: (1) identifying the risks to which the organization is exposed; (2) assessing the probability of a particular risk occurring, and the resulting consequences; (3) selecting countermeasures, usually on a basis of cost-effectiveness; (4) drawing up contingency measures; and (5) monitoring and periodically reviewing these arrangements. (Bibliographic Abstract only)

Eshragh, F. and Mamdani, E.H. A General Approach to Linguistic Approximation, *International Journal of Man-Machine Studies,* vol. 11, (1979), 501-519. (Reprinted in [Mamdani and Gaines, 1981]).

One of the most difficult problems associated with the modeling of natural languague computations with the operations of fuzzy sets is the description of a derived fuzzy set by an appropriate natural language expression. In this paper Eshragh and Mamandi describe a system they have constructed that performs this mapping (called the "translation back into linquistics" by some less precise authors). The solution they propose is especially germane to the use of fuzzy sets as the models of natural language expressions in the areas of risk analysis (a "soft" application area, as opposed to, for example, controller design, a "hard" application area). (see [Pappis and Mamdani, 1977] for more details of the use of fuzzy notions in "hard" areas.) The algorithm of Eshragh and Mandani appears to be vastly superior to the algorithm now used in the Fuzzy Risk Analyzer at the George Washington Univeristy and described in Clements [1977]. They have also included in their algorithm a general method for the reduction of expressions like "NOT ABOVE X AND NOT BELOW X" to "X", a tremendous improvement especially when such a system is to be used by people unfamiliar with the inner workings of the fuzzy models of natural language expressions.

Feagans, T.B. and Biller, W.F. Fuzzy Concepts in the Analysis of Public Health Risks, in *Fuzzy Sets-Theory and Applications to Policy Analysis and Information Systems,* Paul Wang and S.K. Chang (Eds.) Publ. Corp. Plenum, New York, (1980) p. 391-404.

This paper is a discussion of the inherent imprecision in many of the variables involved in estimating risks to the public health. One interesting question raised is whether to model the imprecision of such variables, or to artifically induce precision by not modeling the fuzziness. The authors state that this decision in itself is fuzzy.

Fine, L.H. Computer Center Security. Assessing the Degree of Risk, *Computerweek*, vol. 2, no. 20, (May 1979), 6-7.

There is no such thing as 100% security and, in the final analysis, security depends on the individuals in an organization. At the same time, security demands vary from one installation to another and within these, from one specific application to another. It is important to quantify the degree of risk to obtain both management commitment to the security policy and the resources needed to implement it, and also to justify the costs of any potential security plans.

Fischoff, B. Behavioral Aspects of Cost-Benefit Analysis in *Energy Risk Management*, G. Goodman and W. Rowe (Eds.), London: Academic Press, 1979.

An excellent overview of problems in human information handling capacity which bear on cost/benefit estimation, such as risk analysis. Fischoff states that:

> A rather robust result is that people have a great deal of difficulty both in comprehending information under conditions of complexity and uncertainty and in making valid inferences from such information. The fallibility of such judgement stems in part from the counter-intuitive nature of many probabilistic processes, in part from the lack of hands-on experience with low probability and high consequence events, and in part from the mental overload created by many problems.

Fox, J. Towards a Reconciliation of Fuzzy Logic and Standard Logic, *International Journal of Man-Machine Studies*, vol. 15, (1981), 213-220.

A reply to the arguments of Haack [Haack, 1979] that fuzzy logic is an abomination. Fox argues from three different approaches that fuzzy logic is necessary. He then attempts to reconcile some of the conflicting views of Haack and Zadeh.

Franksen, O.I. Fuzzy Sets, Subjective Measurements, and Utility, *International Journal of Man-Machine Studies*, vol. 11, no. 4, (July 1979), 521-545.

Fuzzy reasoning is founded on subjective measurements specified as grades of membership of property categories called fuzzy sets. The membership gradings, it is assumed, may be expressed numerically by functions or corresponding discrete representations, the values of which submit to the conventional arithmetic operations. This paper raises the question as to the empirical justification of these assumptions. That is, what empirical support can be established for this approach considering the properties of subjective measurements in psychophysics and those of utility in modern microeconomics or management science. (Bibliographic Abstract only)

Freeling, A.N.S. Fuzzy Sets and Decision Analysis, *IEEE Transactions on Systems, Man, and Cybernetics*, vol. SMC-10, no. 7, (July 1980), 341-354.

The applicability of fuzzy set theory to decision analysis is examined. This work extends the ideas in Watson *et al.* [1979]. Particular emphasis is placed on justifying the use of Zadeh's fuzzy calculus to model impression, and an axiomatic system is suggested toward this end. This is seen as an attempt at extending Savage's axioms of subjective probability to produce approximate probabilities. It is argued that the method proposed in Watson *et al.*, [1979] for comparing decision options is unsatisfactory, and several alternative methods are developed. Some computational anomalies are pointed out which severely limit the potential of this methodology. It is suggested that, for individual decision-making, fuzzy decision analysis should be viewed as an automatic sensitivity analysis, but that fuzzy sets may be useful with another interpretation for group decision-making. The conclusisons are that the methodology has too many limitations to be of use for isolated decisions but that it may have a value for often repeated generic decisions. (Bibliographic Abstract only)

Gaines, B.R. Foundations of Fuzzy Reasoning, in *Fuzzy Automata and Decision Processes*, Madan M. Gupta, George N. Saridis, and Brian R. Gaines (Eds.), New York: Elsevier North-Holland, (1977), 19–75.

In this paper, Gaines presents a comprehensive introduction to the use of fuzzy sets to formally model human cognition and reasoning. This paper is organized in a similar manner to this text with major sections on the basics of fuzzy set theory, operations on fuzzy sets, hedges, etc. Gaines's treatment is considerably more scholarly and more mathematical than that here and also provides a wealth of historical motivation for many of the topics we have touched on.

——— and Kohout, L.J. The Fuzzy Decade: A Bibliography of Fuzzy Systems and Closely Related Topics, *International Journal of Man-Machine Studies*, vol. 9, no. 1, (1977), 1–68.

Giles, R. A Formal System for Fuzzy Reasoning, *Fuzzy Sets and Systems*, vol. 2, no. 3, (1979), 233–257.

A formal system for fuzzy reasoning is described which is capable of dealing rationally with evidence which may be inconsistent and/or involve degrees of belief. The basic idea is that the meaning of each formal sentence should be given by a certain commitment or bet associated with it. Each view of evidence is first expressed in the form of such a (hypothetical) bet, which is then written as a formal sentence in a language related to Lukasiewicz logic. The sentences may be weighted to express the relative reliability of the various informants. A detailed account is given of the procedures by which an arbitrary sentence in common language can be translated into a formal sentence. (Bibliographic Abstract only)

———, A Computer Program for Fuzzy Reasoning, *Fuzzy Sets and Systems*, vol. 4, no. 3, (1980), 221–234.

An interactive computer program is described which implements the procedure proposed in Giles, [1979]. The problem in question is that of deciding what conclusions may be drawn in the presence of (possibly conflicting) evidence provided, generally with associated partial degrees of belief, by several sources of differing reliability. In using the program, each piece of evidence is entered as a sentence (using the terms

NOT, AND, OR, and IMPLIES as necessary), with an associated 'degree of belief' and 'weight'; followed by a tentative conclusion. The system returns the degree(s) of belief and weight(s) which may rationally be attached to the conclusion. (Bibliographic Abstract only)

Goguen, J.A. Concept Representation in Natural and Artificial Languages: Axioms, Extensions, and Applications for Fuzzy Sets, *International Journal of Man-Machine Studies*, vol. 6, (1974), 513-561. (Reprinted in [Mamdani and Gaines, 1981])

In this paper Goguen presents an axiomatic basis for fuzzy set theory based on the theory of categories, a more basic and more abstract theory than the theory of (ordinary) sets.

———, Fuzzy Sets and the Social Nature of Truth, in *Advances in Fuzzy Set Theory and Applications*, Gupta, M.M., Ragade, R.K. and Yager, R.R. (Eds.), New York: Elsevier North-Holland, (1979), 49-67.

A philosophical discussion of questions about fuzzy set theory (e.g., "Is it a paradox that the 'degree of membership' used to indicate a degree of uncertainty is itself very precisely given as a real number?") and the implications of fuzzy set theory to the currently held theory of truth.

Gupta, M.M., Ragade, R.K. and Yager, R.R. (Eds.), *Advances in Fuzzy Set Theory and Applications*, New York: Elsevier North-Holland, Inc., (1979).

Fuzzy set theory has made it possible to characterize the pervasive reality of fuzziness and vagueness in human thought processes. This work contains over 30 papers involving over 45 researchers from all the major institutions around the world involved in the development of this exponentially growing field. It introduces the basic concepts in the theory, and describes the research trends both in theory and applications. The most up-to-date bibliography containing over 1,800 references is appended to this work.

Papers from this work which are included in this annotated bibliography are:

An Example of Linguistic Modeling: The Case of Mulder's Theory of Power— [Kickert, 1979]

Some Properties of Fuzzy Numbers—[Mizumoto and Tanaka, 1979]

Fuzzy Sets and the Social Nature of Truth—[Goguen, 1979]

Fuzzy Propositional Approach to Psycholinguistic Problems: An Application of Fuzzy Set Theory to Cognitive Science—[Oden, 1979]

Exploring Linguistic Consequences of Assertions in Social Sciences—[Wenstop, 1979]

Effects of Context on Fuzzy Membership Functions—[Hersh, Caramazza, and Brownell, 1979]

———, Saridis, G.N. and Gaines, B.R. (Eds.), *Fuzzy Automata and Decision Processes*, New York: Elsevier North-Holland, (1977).

Papers from this work which are included in this bibliography are:

Progress in Modeling of Human Reasoning by Fuzzy Logic—[Kaufmann, 1977]

Fuzzy Set Theory—A Perspective—[Zadeh, 1977B]

Foundations of Fuzzy Reasoning—[Gaines, 1977]

'Fuzzy-ism'—The First Decade—[Gupta, 1977]

———, Fuzzy-ism'—The First Decade, in *Fuzzy Automata and Decision Processes*, Gupta, M.M., Saridis, G.N. and Gaines, B.R. (Eds.), New York: Elsevier North-Holland, (1977).

Haack, S. Do we need 'fuzzy logic'?, *International Journal of Man-Machine Studies*, vol. 11, (1979), 437–445.

Haack argues that the introduction of fuzzy variables into logic, for example, the notion that a logical variable takes its values from a set of natural language expressions like TRUE, RATHER TRUE, EXTREMELY TRUE, NOT VERY TRUE, etc., with these expressions then in turn modeled by fuzzy sets, is an abomination. She reasons that this approach robs logic of its very reason for existence: extreme and total precision. Haack further argues that many of the desired results of the so-called "fuzzy logic" can be achieved using "ordinary" many-valued logics.

Heider, E.R. *On the Internal Structure of Perceptual and Semantic Categories*, Unpublished paper, Department of Psychology, University of California, Berkeley, (1971).

Hersh, H.M. and Caramazza, A. A Fuzzy Set Approach to Modifiers and Vagueness in Natural Language, *Journal of Experimental Psychology: General*, vol. 105, no. 3, (1976), 254–276.

This paper describes the results of an experiment to determine the degree of correlation of the natural, inherent, and intuitive meanings of some imprecise natural language expressions and the formal and exact meaning given to those expressions in Zadeh's fuzzy set theory. It is suggested that with only two exceptions Zadeh's theory is a reasonably accurate model of the way humans perceive fuzzy notions. Of the two exceptions, one is a general caveat for all fuzzy expressions and the other is specific to the fuzzy modifier "very." The general caveat is that there appear to be two *modes* in which humans interpret fuzzy expressions: logical mode and idiomatic mode. Zadeh's theory models only the logical mode. The specific exception to the interpretation of the fuzzy modifier "very" is an alternate interpretation to Zadeh's intensification operator—an alternate interpretation that appears to better model the actual human usage of the word "very." (See also [Macvicar-Whelen, 1978] and [Rubin, 1979].)

————, ————, and Brownell, H.H. Effects of Context on Fuzzy Membership Functions, in *Advances in Fuzzy Set Theory and Applications*, Gupta, M.M., Ragade, R.K. and Yager, R.R. (Eds.), New York, Elsevier North-Holland, (1979), 389-408.

The meaning for many vague terms appears to vary with context. For example, consider the meaning for the word "small" in "small mouse" and "small elephant." When one is attempting to define the membership function for a fuzzy set interpretation of the semantics of such a term, it is important to take into account such contextual effects. In this paper some of the effects of context are described and measured experimentally. A subproblem that is also addressed in detail in this paper is that of determining if two tentative membership functions differ substantially. A sophisticated mathematical solution to this question is provided.

Hoffman, L.J., Michelman, E.H. and Clements, D. SECURATE—Security Evaluation and Analysis Using Fuzzy Metrics, *Proceedings of the 1978 National Computer Conference*, vol. 47, AFIPS Press, Montvale, New Jersey, (1978), 531-540.

The authors have described an interactive security evaluation system which uses fuzzy metrics. The system models the installation to be analyzed as a set of object-threat-feature triples. The associated measures—object values, threat likelihoods, and feature resistance—are then used as input to security evaluation functions. The user specifies these features in terms of "fuzzy" linguistic variables. The system, implemented in APL, was programmed on an Amdahl 470 computer.

———— and Neitzel, L.A. Inexact Analysis of Risk, *Proceedings of the IEEE 1980 International Conference on Cybernetics and Society*, Boston, Massachusetts, 8-10 October 1980; reprinted in *Computer Security Journal*, vol. 1, no. 1, (Spring 1981), 61-72.

A fundamental paper on the use of fuzzy natural language expressions to estimate the risk associated with a particular system. Such a scheme is particularly appropriate when there is an absence of sufficient data for statistical prediction, e.g., in the evaluation of the security of a data processing facility.

Information Policy, Inc., IPIRISK User Manual, Washington, D.C., (1981).

Jain, R. Decision Making in the Presence of Fuzziness and Uncertainty, *Proceedings of the 1977 IEEE Conference on Decision and Control*, (Published by the IEEE, Piscataway, N.J.), (1977), 1318-1323.

The concept of fuzzy sets is being increasingly utilized to deal with ill-defined terms and variables. Methods have been proposed to find the optimal alternative in the presence of fuzzy variables. In this paper, a method for finding the optimal alternative in the presence of both the fuzziness and the uncertainty is presented. The method deals with those situations in which the ratings of the alternatives are known imprecisely and the state of the system is known with uncertainty. The impreciseness of the ratings is presented using fuzzy sets and the expected fuzzy rating for each alternative is calculated. (Bibliographic Abstract only)

———, Fuzzyism and Real World Problems, in *Fuzzy Sets—Theory and Applications to Policy Analysis and Information Systems—Proceedings of the Symposium on Policy Analysis and Information Systems,* Wang, P.P. and Chang, S.K. (Eds.), Durham, North Carolina, 28–30 June 1980, New York: Plenum Publ. Corp. (1980), 129–132.

In this paper Jain argues that too much research in fuzzy set theory is concerned only with proving more and more abstract properties of fuzzy sets rather than in applying fuzzy sets to non-trivial real world problems. He then outlines some mathematically unattractive but practically important areas of fuzzy set theory: membership function selection, fuzzy operators, and fuzzy operators, and fuzzy algorithms. (Bibliographic Abstract only)

Johannsen, G. and Rouse, W.B. Mathematical Concepts for Modeling Human Behavior in Complex Man-Machine Systems, *Human Factors*, vol. 21, no. 6, (December 1979), 733–747.

Many useful mathematical models for manual control, monitoring, and decision-making tasks in man-machine systems have been designed and successfully applied. However, critical comments have occasionally been made, mainly by practitioners concerned with the design of complex man-machine systems. They especially blame models which seem to explain only data from abstract subtask experiments designed particularly for these models. In this review paper, an initial approach to bridging the gap between these two perspectives of models is presented. From the manifold of possible human tasks, a very popular baseline scenario has been chosen, namely car driving. A hierarchy of human activities is derived by analyzing this task in general terms. A structural description leads to a block diagram and a time-sharing computer analogy. The range of applicability of existing mathematical models is considered with respect to the hierarchy of human activities in real, complex tasks. Also other mathematical descriptions at least briefly considered here include utility, estimation, control, queueing and fuzzy set theory as well as artificial intelligence techniques. Some thoughts are given as to how these methods might be integrated and how further work might be pursued. (Bibliographic Abstract only)

Kandel, A.M., Fuzzy Statistics and Forecast Evaluation, *IEEE Transactions on Systems, Man, and Cybernetics*, vol. SMC-8, no. 5, (May 1978), 396–400.

The author reports on the development of analytical methods which enable him to investigate subjective evaluations by utilizing qualitative fuzzy techniques. By extending the axiomatic basis of probability theory, he derives a natural way of expressing the central tendency of a data set via the concept of the fuzzy expected value. The fuzzy statistics developed here give the author the power to investigate a concept of "average" which is based on the natural and subjective view of "real world" analysis, as reflected by the theory of fuzzy sets, and more particularly, fuzzy analytical techniques. (Bibliographic Abstract only)

Kaufmann, A., *Introduction to the Theory of Fuzzy Sets*—vol. 1, New York: Academic Press, 1975.

————, Progress in Modeling of Human Reasoning by Fuzzy Logic, in *Fuzzy Automata and Decision Processes*, Gupta, M.M., Saridis, G.N. and Gaines, B.R. (Eds.), New York: Elsevier North-Holland, (1977), 11-77.

A comprehensive review of topics in fuzzy set theory currently being applied to the problem of modeling human cognition and decision making activities with a particular emphasis on extensions/generalizations to fuzzy set theory in that application area.

Kickert, J.M. An Example of Linguistic Modeling: The Case of Mulder's Theory of Power, in *Advances in Fuzzy Set Theory and Applications*, Gupta, M.M., Ragade, R.K. and Yager, R.R. (Eds.), New York: Elsevier North-Holland, (1979), 519-540.

This paper presents a detailed example of the use of linguistic variables and fuzzy reasoning in the modeling (for the purpose of computer simulation) of theories in the social sciences. The general conclusion of Kickert is that such modeling is useful and that other application studies should be performed.

Kochen, M., and Badre, A.N. On the Precision of Adjectives which denote Fuzzy Sets, *Journal of Cybernetics*, vol. 4, no. 1, (1974), 49-59.

This paper describes a method for measuring the imprecision of a given adjective in a sentence and the use of this method for comparing the precision of adjectives as well as the consistency of such comparisons over trials.

————, Applications of Fuzzy Sets in Psychology, in *Fuzzy Sets and Their Applications to Cognitive and Decision Processes*, Zadeh, L.A. Fu, K.S. Tanaka, K. and Shimura, M. (Eds.), New York, Academic Press, (1975), 395-408.

In this paper Kochen briefly reviews the manner in which fuzzy set theory has been used in psychology. His analysis of these uses and the corresponding results is that the population can be divided into three classes of people and that fuzzy set theory may be an appropriate mathematical basis for describing the behavior of one of these classes. This class, labeled by Kochen as "estimators" (as opposed to "thresholders" and "reliables") comprises about half of the population.

Koksalan, M.M. and Dagli, H.C. A Fuzzy Programming Approach to Departmental Planning, Technical Report, Middle East Technical University, Ankara, Turkey, (1981); (Also presented at the CORS/TIMS/ORSA Joint National Meeting, Toronto, Ontario, 3-6 May 1981).

This paper discusses a fuzzy linear programming solution to the scheduling of classes and instructors in a university department. Initial attempts to use the standard fuzzy set-theoretic operators resulted in only suboptimal solutions, so the authors modified the definitions of the fuzzy intersection as follows: Let A and B be two fuzzy sets

$$A = \{a(x)/x \mid x \in U\}$$
$$B = \{b(x)/x \mid x \in U\}$$

then the "new" fuzzy intersection is

$$A \cap B = \{ \; min(a(x), b(x)) + ca(x) + cb(x) \mid x \; \epsilon \; U \}$$

where c is a "small" constant.

While this new definition of the intersection provided better solutions to the scheduling problem being worked on by the authors, no discussion is provided as to whether or not other applications would benefit from this modified definition, nor is any theoretical justification for the modification given.

Koppelaar, H. and Van Der Linden, G. Linguistic Modelling with APL, *APL 80—International Conference on APL*, 24-26 June 1980, Leiden, Netherlands, Amsterdam: North-Holland, (1980), 183-190.

This paper deals with a relatively new kind of modeling for social processes: linguistic modeling. The new method makes use of linguistic variables and linguistic causal relationships instead of numerical variables and relations which are usual in social systems modeling and simulation. The whole approach is based on the theory of fuzzy sets and is programmed with APL functions. (Bibliographic Abstract only)

Lakoff, G., Hedges: A Study in Meaning Criteria and the Logic of Fuzzy Concept, *Journal of Philosophical Logic*, vol. 2, (1973), 458-508.

An examination of the notion of fuzziness from the point of view of philosophy and linguistics and an assessment of the extent to which Zadeh's fuzzy set theory captures these notions.

Lientz, B.P., *Analysis of Complex, Softly Defined Problems*, (September 1977), (Available from NTIS, #AD-A044 846/4GA.

Softly defined problems are problems in which constraints and objectives are imprecise and fuzzy in the sense of the concepts of fuzzy set theory. A concept of fuzzy worth is formulated. An algorithm is presented which extracts the most worthy alternatives. A method is developed for obtaining all efficient solutions in the neighborhood of several most worthy alternatives. (Bibliographic Abstract only)

Macvicar-Whelen, P.J., Fuzzy Sets, the Concept of Height, and the Hedge "Very" *IEEE Transactions on Systems, Man, and Cybernetics*, Volume SMC-8, no. 6, (June 1978), 507-511.

An experimental and theoretical study of the categorization of human height is reported. Subjects of both sexes whose ages ranged from 6 to 72 were asked to classify the height of both men and women using the labels 'Very Very Short', 'Very Short', 'Short', 'Tall', 'Very Tall', and 'Very Very Tall'. The experimental results confirm Zadeh's contention about the existence of fuzzy classification (the lack of sharp borders for the classes) but indicate that the hedge 'Very' causes a shift of the class frontier rather than a steepening of the membership function proposed by Zadeh. As a result of the experimental studies, a new modeling of the classification process in terms of a family of high- and low-pass filters is proposed. (Bibliographic Abstract only) (See also [Hersh and Caramazza, 1976])

Mamdani, E.H. and Gaines, B.R. *Fuzzy Reasoning and Its Applications*, New York: Academic Press, (1981).

A collection of papers from the International Journal of Man-Machine Studies. Those that appear in this bibliography are:

PRUF - A Meaning Representation Language for Natural Languages—[Zadeh, 1978]

Concept Representation in Natural and Artificial Languages: Axioms, Extensions, and Applications for Fuzzy Sets—[Goguen, 1974]

Fuzzy Logic and Fuzzy Reasoning—[Baldwin, 1979B]

Deductive Verbal Models of Organizations—[Wenstop, 1976]

A General Approach to Linguistic Approximation—[Eshraugh and Mamdani, 1979]

On Foundations of Reasoning with Uncertain Facts and Vague Concepts—[Schefe, 1980]

McCLoskey, M.E. and Glucksberg, S. Natural Categories: Well Defined or Fuzzy Sets?, *Memory and Cognition*, vol. 6, no. 4, (1978), 462–472.

There currently exist two promiment schools of thought on the subject of cognitive memory and more generally on the notion of concept formation. One school assumes the existence of well defined and delimited natural categories where category membership is total—an entity is either completely in the category or it is completely out of the category. The other school assumes that most natural categories are inherently vague in nature and that category membership is a matter of degree. McCloskey and Glucksberg strongly suggest that the second school of thought is more consistent with the way people ordinarily deal with categories, as measured by their experiments. Such work would imply that many of the concepts/categories fundamental to the analysis of risk are fuzzy and that, therefore, fuzzy set theory is a more appropriate theoretical base for risk analysis than traditional set theory.

Meadows, C. Identifying the Greatest Contributor to Risk in a Tree Model, Department of Electrical Engineering and Computer Science, The George Washington University, Washington, D.C., Technical Report GWU-IIST-81-09, 1 May 1981.

Milling, P. Fuzzy Variables in Computer Simulation Modelling, *Proceedings of the International Conference on Cybernetics and Society*, 8–10 October 1980, Boston, Published by the IEEE, (1980), 1–6.

A frequently encountered problem in the process of developing computer simulation models is the transformation of mainly verbal or qualitative information into the precise syntax of a program. A promising approach to bridge the gap between the technically necessary precision and the empirically more appropriate, but imprecise, description of the problem under investigation is offered by the mathematical theory of fuzzy sets. This approach is discussed and analyzed with respect to its applicability to social system modeling. (Bibliographic Abstract only)

Mizumoto, M. Properties of Fuzzy Sets under Various Operations, *Transactions of the IECE of Japan*, vol. E-64, no. 3, 183–189.

Among the basic operations which can be performed on fuzzy sets are the operations of union, intersection, complement, algebraic product and algebraic sum. In addition to these operations, new operations called "bounded-sum" and "bounded-difference" were defined by L.A. Zadeh to investigate fuzzy reasoning. This paper investigates the algebraic properties of fuzzy sets under these new operations of bounded-sum and bounded-difference, as well as the properties under the well-known operations of union, intersection, algebraic product and algebraic sum combined with the operations of bounded-sum and bounded-difference. (Translation of author's abstract)

—— and Tanaka, K. Some Properties of Fuzzy Numbers, in *Advances in Fuzzy Set Theory and Applications*, Gupta, M.M., Ragade, R.K., and Yager, R.R. (Eds.), New York: Elsevier North-Holland, (1979), 153–164.

This paper explores the algebraic properties of fuzzy numbers such as "ABOUT 2" or "MOREORLESS 7", under the operations of addition, subtraction, multiplication, and division. All of these operations are defined for fuzzy sets through the application of Zadeh's extension principle. Among the results of Mizumoto and Tanaka is the following theorem and corollary, important to the operation of the Fuzzy Risk Analyzer:

Thm: If A and B are convex fuzzy numbers on the real line R, then $A + B$, $A - B$, and $A \times B$ are also convex fuzzy numbers.

Cor: This theorem does not, in general, hold for discrete fuzzy numbers.

Nagy, T.J. and Hoffman, L.J. Exploratory Evaluation of the Accuracy of Linguistic vs. Numeric Risk Assessment of Computer Security, Technical Report GWU-IIST-81-07, Computer Security Research Group, The George Washington University, May 1981.

This exploratory study determined that the benefits of using natural language estimates as opposed to numerical estimates are pronounced. It is hypothesized that the use of such natural language estimates reduces the occurrences of extremely inaccurate numerical estimates, thereby improving the estimates of the "average" risk analyst/computer security consultant.

Nguyen, H.T., Mathematical Tools for Linguistic Probabilities, *Proceedings of the 1977 IEEE Conference on Decision and Control*, Piscataway, New Jersey, (1977), 1345–1350.

Transformations of fuzzy sets are discussed using the relation between random sets and fuzzy sets. The author proposes the general formulation of optimization under elastic constraints. This formulation is based upon the notion of maximizing and minimizing sets. Using this formulation, he justifies the extension problem of possibility measures to fuzzy sets. (Bibliographic Abstract only)

————, Some Mathematical Tools for Linguistic Probabilities, *Fuzzy Sets and Systems*, vol. 2, no. 1, (1979), 53-65.

In this paper, Nguyen proposes and develops some concepts and techniques useful for the theory of linguistic probabilities introduced by Zadeh. These probabilities are expressed in linguistic rather than numerical terms. The mathematical framework for this study is based upon the possibility theory. The author first formulates the problem of optimization under elastic constraints, which is not only important for mathematical programming but will serve to justify the extension of possibility measure to linguistic variables. Next, in connection with translation rules in natural languages, the author studies some transformations of fuzzy sets using a relation between random sets and fuzzy sets. Finally, the author points out some differences between random variables and fuzzy variables, and presents the mathematical notion of possibility, in the setting of set-functions, as a special case of Choquet capacities. (Bibliographic Abstract only)

Oden, G.C., Integration of Fuzzy Logical Information, *Journal of Experimental Psychology: Human Perception and Performance*. vol. 3, no. 4, (1977), 565-575.

The extension of some of the basic operations of ordinary set theory to that of fuzzy set theory is a task that can be undertaken from a number of different points of view. Bellman and Giertz, as well as Yager, undertake this task from a mathematical point of view [Bellman and Giertz, 1973], [Yager, 1979]. In this paper Oden pursues this question from a psychological point of view. His psychological studies strongly suggest that, instead of Zadeh's definition of the intersection of two fuzzy sets as

$$A \cap B = \{ min(a(x), b(x))/x \mid x \in U\},$$

the following definition is one which better fits the way people actually manipulate fuzzy concepts:

$$A \cap B = \{ a(x) * b(x) \mid x \in U\}$$

This second rule appears to better fit the experimental data when A and B are not "independent." The differences between these two rules can be demonstrated by considering the following two examples of logical reasoning concerning the fuzzy set *young people*. If John is in the set *young people* with plausibility .9 and Mary is in the set with plausibility .7, then it seems quite reasonable (and, in fact, is experimentally observed) that the plausibility of *both* John and Mary being in the set *young people* is $min(.9, .7) = .7$. Thus, the intersection operator (which is often expressed in English as "and") appears to be accurately modeled by the minimum operator. An example which is not modeled well by the minimum operator is the concatenation of the following intuitively clear statements: "A one-day old infant is in the set *young people* with plausibility 1.0" and "If someone is in the set *young people* one day, then he is in the set the next day with plausibility .99." The paradox occurs when one considers the statement "A one-day old infant is young *and* living another day doesn't destroy one's youth *and* living another day doesn't destroy one's youth *and* ...." By the minimum rule the infant will always be in the set *young people*—even when the infant is 60 years old! The multiplicative rule, however, more accurately reflects reality.

Oden concludes with:

> It has long been recognized that standard formal logic provides a poor description of the processes of actual human thought and that this is in large part because traditional logic is completely discrete and adheres strictly to the principle of the excluded middle: a statement must either be true or false. Clearly this principle does not characterize much of our subjective experience and knowledge. ... Clearly, however, before such theories of fuzzy semantic information processing may be formulated in any detail, it will be necessary to have a much better understanding of the nature of the basic cognitive processes dealing with fuzzy information. (There is a need for) the development of such a model of fuzzy psycho-logic.

———, Fuzzy Propositional Approach to Psycholinguistic Problems: An Application to Fuzzy Set Theory in Cognitive Science, in *Advances in Fuzzy Set Theory and Applications*, Gupta, M.M., Ragade, R.K. and Yager, R.R. (Eds). New York: Elsevier North-Holland, (1979).

In this paper Oden proposes a fuzzy propositional model of human semantic information processing. The basic structure of the model is that of a propositional network of semantic concepts where the primitive semantic relations are fuzzy predicates (as defined in Zadeh, [1975 (Part II)]. He then describes some of the experimental basis for this model, demonstrating the competency of humans to process fuzzy concepts and the manner in which they process them.

Okuda, T., Tanaka, H. and Asa, K. Formulation of Fuzzy Decision Problems with Fuzzy Information using Probability Measures of Fuzzy Events, *Information and Control*, vol. 38, no. 2, (August 1978), 135-147.

For decision problems in the real world, states of nature, information, and actions should be viewed as fuzzy events. The application of fuzzy set theory and the statistical design theory to the decision problems in fuzzy events leads to a specific formulation of fuzzy decision problems and the definitions of entropy, worth of information, and quantity of information. Some results which are analogous to those in the statistical decision theory are given in this paper. (Bibliographic Abstract only)

Papis, C.P. and Mamdani, E.H. A Fuzzy Logic Controller for a Traffic Junction, *IEEE Transactions on Systems, Man, and Cybernetics*, vol. SMC-7, no. 10, (October 1977), 707-717.

Work done on the implementation of a fuzzy logic controller in a single intersection of two one-way streets is presented. The model of the intersection is described and validated, and the use of the theory of fuzzy sets in constructing a controller based on linguistic control intersections is introduced. The results obtained from the implementation of the fuzzy logic controller are tabulated against those corresponding to a conventional effective vehicle-actuated controller. With the performance criterion being the average delay of vehicles, it is shown that the use of a fuzzy logic controller results in better performance.

Procyk, T. J. and Mamdani, E.H. Linguistic Self-Organizing Process Controller, *Automatica*, vol. 15, no. 1, (January 1979), 15-30.

In this paper, a heuristic controller for dynamic processes is presented whose control policy is able to develop and improve automatically. The controller's heuristics take the form of a set of linguistic decision rules which are expressed quantitatively and manipulated by using the theory of fuzzy sets. A series of experiments are described which show that the controller can be applied to a wide range of different processes which can be multivariable and also non-linear and demonstrate the controller's robustness. (Bibliographic Abstract only)

Rajkovic, V. and Efstathiou, J. Multiattribute Decision Making Using a Fuzzy Heuristic Approach, *IEEE Transactions on Systems, Man, and Cybernetics,* vol. SMC-9, no. 6, (June 1979), 326-333.

Multiattribute decision making (DM) is treated as a special kind of structured human problem solving. Emphasis is placed on the use of the available knowledge about utilities, which is obtained by combining heuristics and traditional aggregation methods. In this way, the problem of partial utilities and their interdependence may be solved. A fuzzy approach to DM is described, incorporating linguistic variables, relations, and algorithms. It is summarized in a formal model and illustrated by an example. (Bibliographic Abstract only)

Rine, D.C. Possibility Theory: A Tool for Analyzing Computer Security, *Proceedings of the Ninth International Symposium on Multiple-Valued Logic,* 29-31 May 1979, Bath, England, Published by the IEEE, (1979), 208-221.

In this paper the author continues the investigation initiated in a previous paper of correlations between computer security specifications and protection techniques in order to find computer-assisted ways, such as those appearing in the paper, by which features of a computer system involving security specifications may be designed or evaluated. The development of a model based on a theory of possibilities and fuzzy sets is continued from the previous paper, and an APL implementation is also included as a new development toward computer-assisted tools. (Bibliographic Abstract only)

Robertson, S.E. Nature of Fuzz: A Diatribe, *Journal of the American Society of Information Science (J. ASIS),* vol. 29, no. 6, November 1978, 304-307.

The imprecision of some of the concepts which are used in formal models in information science has led to a spate of attempts to apply fuzzy set theory to aspects of information science. An analysis of the various kinds of imprecision that can occur indicates strongly that fuzzy set theory is not an appropriate formalism for these models. (Bibliographic Abstract only)

Rouse, W.B. Model of Human Decision Making in Fault Diagnosis Tasks that Include Feedback and Redundancy, *IEEE Transactions on Systems, Man, and Cybernetics*, vol. SMC-9, no. 4(April 1979), 237–240.

A previously reported model of human decision making in fault diagnosis is extended to include situations where feedback and component redundancy are important considerations. The model is based on concepts from the theory of fuzzy sets. The results of an experiment with human subjects are reported and used to estimate the parameters of the model. (Bibliographic Abstract only)

———, *Systems Engineering Models of Human-Machine Interactions*, New York: North-Holland, 1980.

This study of a number of mathematical models for the interaction between man and machine includes one chapter on the use of fuzzy set theory in the modeling of "situations where the human must cope with an inexact knowledge of the process being observed and/or controlled."

Rubin, D.C. On Measuring Fuzziness: A Comment on 'A Fuzzy Set Approach to Modifiers and Vagueness in Natural Languages', *Journal of Experimental Psychology: General*, vol. 108, no. 4, (1979), 486–489.

In this short paper, Rubin criticizes the methods of Hersh and Caramazza (as presented in Hersh and Caramazza [1976]) but not their results. According to Rubin, the experimental design used by Hersh and Caramazza introduced the appropriate amount of "fuzziness," rather than that fuzziness being reflected by the inherent imprecision of natural language expressions and their use. Rubin improved the experimental design, re-ran the experiments and came to approximately the same conclusion as Hersh and Caramazza.

Schefe, P. On Foundations of Reasoning with Uncertain Facts and Vague Concepts, *International Journal of Man-Machine Studies*, vol. 12, no. 1, (January 1980), 35–62. (Reprinted in [Mamdani and Gaines, 1981])

This paper contains an outline of a probabilistic foundation of multi-valued "fuzzy" reasoning. The fundamental concept is "agreement probability." It is shown that some undesirable consequences of "fuzzy logic," e.g., that tautologies of propositional calculus are not preserved, can be avoided. A proposal for alternative definitions of "degree of membership" and operations on membership-graded sets is given. "Fuzziness" is interpreted as a subjective concept, i.e., subjective uncertainty pertaining to the truth of a proposition. An important consequence thereof is that, from a graded agreement associated with a conjecture, an agreement degree pertaining to its negation cannot be computed. Zadeh's conjecture that truth value can be equated with membership degrees is shown to be inadequate. Alternative interpretation of the linguistic phenomena considered and of the Sorites paradox are given. Especially, the meta-linguistic character of the phenomena is emphasized. It is argued that "vagueness" and "uncertainty" should be clearly distinguished as well as "possibility" and "applicability." Suggestions are made how underlying measuring scales and orderings of objects are used in reasoning processes involving vague concepts.

Shaket, E., *Fuzzy Semantics for a Natural-Like Language Defined over a World of Blocks*, M.S. Thesis, University of California at Los Angeles, 1975.

This thesis describes an APL implementation of a natural language understanding system similar to that of the famous SHRDLU system by Winograd (Winograd, Terry, *Understanding Natural Language*, New York: Academic Press, 1972) with the extension of modeling fuzzy statements. An example of a type of noun phrase that Shaket's system can correctly resolve is "The large, rather green block which is very near a small blue cube on top of a very large red-orange slab."

Sheppard, D. The Adequacy of Everyday Quantitative Expressions as Measurements of Qualities, *British Journal of Psychology*, vol. 45, (1954), 40–50.

A pre-fuzzy set theory experiment to determine the applicability of natural language expressions (as opposed to numerical estimates) for quality measurement.

Stern, L. Security for your Computer Facility, *Office*, vol. 88, no. 2, (August 1978), 18–21.

Physical security can provide a closed, controlled, safe environment for your computing facility, but it does leave you vulnerable to abuses, thefts, fraud, and internal sabotage. You cannot achieve 100% security because for every security measure you take, a countermeasure can be found. One momentary security lapse or an accidental failure and all may be lost! Physical security is no more than one layer of a multilevel shield which should include: (1) A risk analysis including an evaluation of various potential threats, their probable frequencies, impacts, and the costs of potential damages; (2) Manual, computerized, procedural and organizational controls; (3) Internal and external audits; and (4) Hardware and software protection contingency planning which should be based on formal backup and recovery arrangements. Although ordinary mistakes are the most costly, Stern suggests that one should concentrate only on a few of the common EDP threats: fire, water, malicious acts, and failure of utilities. (Bibliographic Abstract only)

Sticha, P.J., Weiss, J.J. and Donnell, M.L. Evaluation and Integration of Imprecise Information, Technical Report, Decisions and Designs, Inc., McLean, Virginia, (August 1979).

Although fuzzy set theory has been rapidly gaining popularity as a rigorous framework for incorporating imprecision into quantitative reasoning, a survey of existing literature indicates the lack of any consistently applied operational definition for the fundamental concept of membership function. Presently, the membership of an element x in a set S is defined as the degree of truth of the statement 'x is a member of S'. It then becomes necessary to develop an empirically valid scale of truth which allows not only the binary extremes of 'TRUE' and 'FALSE', but also the continuum of intermediate values. In one experiment, subjects performed two tasks: pairwise comparison and direct numerical scaling of the relative truth of simple sentences. Results indicated that (1) the high degree of transitivity in each subject's paired-comparison judgements leads to the rejection of the hypothesis of a simple two-valued TRUE-FALSE logic in favor of a continuum of values; (2) the ability to discriminate, as judged by the consistency between direct ratings and paired-comparison judgements, seems to be uniform along the TRUE-FALSE continuum, again favoring the hypothesis of a continuum of truth values over that of a binary categorical judgement; and (3) the high correlation between an item's aggregate binary preference score for a given subject and that subject's direct rating for the item indicates that at least two different methods of inferring degree of truth are highly consistent. (Bibliographic Abstract only)

Tong, R.M. A Linguistic Approach to Decision Making with Fuzzy Sets, *IEEE Transactions on Systems, Man, and Cybernetics*, vol. SMC-10, no. 11, (1980), 716-723.

A technique for making linguistic decisions is presented. Fuzzy sets are assumed to be an appropriate way of dealing with uncertainty, and it is concluded, therefore, that decisions taken on the basis of such information must themselves be fuzzy. It is inappropriate then to present the decision in numerical form; a statement in natural language is much better. For brevity only a single-stage multi-attribute decision problem is considered. Solutions to such problems are shown using ideas in linguistic approximation and truth qualification. An extensive example illuminates the basic ideas and techniques. (Bibliographic Abstract only)

Tribus, M. Fuzzy Sets and Bayesian Methods Applied to the Problem of Literature Search, *IEEE Transactions on Systems, Man, and Cybernetics*, vol. SMC-10, no. 10, (August 1980), 501-502.

Can fuzzy set theory do anything which cannot be done by Bayesian methods? A way to decide is to compare results when the same practical problem is attempted by the two methods. In this correspondence a problem of literature search previously solved by a fuzzy set theory approach is analyzed by Bayesian methods. (Bibliographic Abstract only)

United States Department of Commerce, National Bureau of Standards, *Guidelines for Automatic Data Processing Risk Analysis*, Federal Information Processing Standards Publication Number 65, (FIPS PUB 65), (1 August 1979).

Wang, P.P. and Chang, S.K. (Eds.), *Fuzzy Sets—Theory and Applications to Policy Analysis and Information Systems*, (Proceedings of the Symposium on Policy Analysis and Information Systems, Duke University, 28–30 June 1980), New York: Plenum Publ. Corp., (1980).

Papers from this collection which are included in this bibliography are:

Fuzzyism and Real World Problems—[Jain, 1980]

New Results about Properties and Semantics of Fuzzy Set-Theoretic Operators—[Dubois and Prade, 1980]

Fuzzy Concepts in the Analysis of Public Health Risks—[Feagans and Biller, 1980]

Watson, S.R., Weiss, J.J. and Donnell, M.L. Fuzzy Decision Analysis, *IEEE Transactions on Systems, Man, and Cybernetics*, vol. SMC-9, no. 1, (January 1979), 1-9.

Imprecision in decision analysis is modeled using fuzzy set theory. Fuzziness on the probabilities and utilities used in a decision analysis implies fuzziness on the outputs. A method is suggested for calculating imprecise, though informative, statements about the attractiveness of the different options, in a decision tree, which depends on the imprecision of the inputs. A general discussion of the advantages and disadvantages of the approach is given. (Bibliographic Abstract only)

Wenstop, F. Deductive Verbal Models of Organizations, *International Journal of Man-Machine Studies*, vol. 8, (1976), 293-321. (Reprinted in [Mamdani and Gaines, 1981])

Wenstop proposes a modeling system very similar to the automated risk analysis utility using natural language expressions as input, with the difference that the ultimate goal of the system is not risk analysis but rather the modeling of the dynamics of organizations. This sytem allows one to input rules like 'The level of interpersonal tension is very similar to the visibility of power relations' and 'The closeness of supervision is considerably higher than before if the difference between goals and results is high, otherwise it is slightly lower'. The modeling system then simulates the system's operation and predicts the value of the various variables that describe the organization.

Except for the differences in the ultimate application area, this system is quite similar to that presented in Clements, [1977].

————, Exploring Linguistic Consequences of Assertions in Social Sciences, in *Advances in Fuzzy Set Theory and Applications*, Gupta, M.M., Ragade, R.K. and Yager, R.R. (Eds.), New York: Elsevier North-Holland, (1979), 501-518.

In this paper Wenstop describes a programming language for the modeling of human behavior in the social sciences. Since the knowledge of such behavior is often in the form of general and approximate statements about loosely defined phenomena, a system using linguistic variables is especially appropriate. Wenstop's language provides such variables based on fuzzy set theory and his system is programmed in APL, a frequent language choice for researchers in fuzzy set theory. The set of natural language expressions modeled in this system is especially rich—in addition to primary terms and hedges it includes *connectives* (e.g., AND, OR, BUT, NOR, PLUS, MINUS), *trend modes* (INCREASINGLY, DECREASINGLY, LINEARLY), and *trend directions* (FALLING, CLIMBING, GROWING) as well as conditionals. Such a system allows the modeling of statements like:

A is below *high* but linearly growing

A is below *high* and not lower than *B*

A will be somewhat higher than *B* if *C* is below upper medium but not low

Yager, R.R. Validation of Fuzzy-Linguistic Models, *Journal of Cybernetics*, vol. 8, no. 1, (Jan/Mar 1978A), 17-30.

This article introduces a procedure for validating models that involve linguistic variables. First Yager discusses Zadeh's extension principle for fuzzy sets. Then he discusses the concept of a linguistic truth variable. Using the concepts developed in these sections, he presents a methodology for validation models involving fuzzy and linguistic variables. This procedure is based upon obtaining the value of a truth variable, indicating how true a model is. (Bibliographic Abstract only)

————, Linguistic Models and Fuzzy Truths, *International Journal of Man-Machine Studies*, vol. 10, no. 5, (September 1978B), 483-494.

In this paper the linguistic value of truth is used to derive a procedure for validation of models. The procedure uses fuzzy set theory to obtain the compatibility between observed data and model-generated data. Of significance is the fact that the data can be in linguistic form. (Bibliographic Abstract only)

————, Fuzzy Sets over the Same Space, *Proceedings of the Joint Automation and Control and Conference*, Philadelphia, 15-20 October 1978, Published by the ISA, (1978), 357-361.

A fuzzy set, differing from an ordinary set, allows degrees of membership rather than the strict Aristotelian yes or no. Therefore, using these sets one can define imprecise ideas in terms of fuzzy sets by degrees of membership of precise objects to fuzzy sets corresponding to the imprecise concepts. In the course of developing a calculus in which to formulate imprecise thought patterns, one sometimes is faced with the problem of finding the membership of one fuzzy set in another fuzzy set. This short paper presents a procedure for obtaining these values when both sets are defined in terms of the same base set. (Bibliographic Abstract only)

————, A Measurement-Informational Discussion of Fuzzy Union and Intersection, *International Journal of Man-Machine Studies*, vol. 11, (1979), 189-200.

Yager argues that from a "measurement and informational transmittal point of view" the only meaningful definitions for the union and the intersection of two fuzzy sets are the definitions given by Zadeh. These definitions are meaningful even if the membership functions associated with the fuzzy sets are only ordinal, i.e., are only relative estimates of the degree of membership, as opposed to absolute estimates. (See [Bellman and Giertz, 1973] for a different approach leading to the same result.)

————, A Linguistic Variable for Importance of Fuzzy Sets, *Journal of Cybernetics*, vol. 10, no. 1-3, (1980), 249-260.

This paper introduces the concept of a linguistic variable for importance. This is done by defining its linguistic values as fuzzy subsets over the set of nonnegative numbers. Furthermore, the author shows how to modify a fuzzy subset by its importance. That is, if A is a fuzzy subset of X, and I is its importance, then A becomes $A/\text{Sup } I/$ which is also a fuzzy subset of X. (Bibliographic Abstract only)

Yao, J.T.P., *An Approach to Damage Assessment to Existing Structures*, Technical Report, Purdue University, School of Civil Engineering, October 1979, (NTIS Accession Number PB80-123482).

Application of fuzzy sets as an alternative and/or supplementary approach to assessing the damage state of existing structures is described. Following occurrence of a hazardous event such as a strong-motion earthquake, voluminous data usually are collected and a simplistic conclusion is issued which transmits scant information to structural engineers concerned with these problems. To correct this situation, the theory of fuzzy sets has been applied to the complex problems of assessing damage to existing structures. Fuzzy sets consist of a mathematical model coupled with provisions for the effect of human factors and construction process and experience. For each factor, the gravity of the adverse effect and its consequence are estimated by experts. The report summarizes the state of the art of damage identification of existing structures and presents the fundamental elements of fuzzy sets and their pilot application to actual structural engineering examples. Finally, an approach using fuzzy sets is formulated and discussed in the hope that such a pilot study will simulate interest in this method among structural engineers. Extensive data, equations, and references are included. (Bibliographic Abstract only)

Yezhkova, I.V. and Pospelov, D.A. Decision Making on Fuzzy Grounds, *Engineering Cybernetics*, vol. 15, no. 6, (November–December 1977), 1-7.

An examination is made of questions of constructing a logic of subjective possibilities. Psychological and linguistic assumptions of the investigation of models of subjective probabilities are critically examined. A connection is established between subjective probabilities and fuzzy frequency estimates expressed by words and word combinations of the type 'rarely,' 'very often', etc. A method is proposed for representing subjective frequency distributions of events on a scale that is universal with respect to the events the values of which are fuzzy frequency estimates of the type indicated. The possibilities of using universal scales in the construction of fuzzy influence schemes are pointed out. (Bibliographic Abstract only)

Zadeh, L.A. Fuzzy Sets, *Information and Control*, vol. 8, (1965), 338-353.

The original paper describing the theory of fuzzy sets.

————, Quantitative Fuzzy Semantics, *Information Sciences*, vol. 3, no. 2, (April 1971), 159-176.

————. A Fuzzy-Set-Theoretic Interpretation of Linguistic Hedges, *Journal of Cybernetics*, vol. 2, no. 3, (1972A), 4-34.

————, Fuzzy Languages and their Relation to Human and Machine Intelligence, *Proceedings of the International Conference on Man and Computer*, Bordeaux, 1970, Published by Karger, (1972B), 130-165.

————, The Concept of a Linguistic Variable and its Application to Approximate Reasoning, *Information Sciences*, vol. 8, no. 3, (1975), 199-249 (Part I), vol. 8, no. 4, (1975), 301-357, (Part II), vol. 9, no. 1, (1975), 43-80 (Part III).

The definitive work on the use of fuzzy sets to model natural language expressions. The theoretical treatment given here to this application of fuzzy sets is both deep and thorough. Several applications of this use of fuzzy sets are also explained.

————, Fu, K.S., Tanaka, K. and Shimura, M. (Eds.), *Fuzzy Sets and Their Application to Cognitive and Decision Processes*, New York: Academic Press, 1975.

The only paper from this work included in this bibliography is:

Applications of Fuzzy Sets in Psychology—[Kochen, 1975]

————, A Fuzzy-Algorithmic Approach to the Definition of Complex or Imprecise Concepts, *International Journal of Man-Machine Studies*, vol. 8, (1976), 249-291.

————, PRUF and Its Application to Inference from Fuzzy Propositions, *Proceedings of the 1977 IEEE Conference on Decision and Control*, New Orleans, (7-9 December 1977A), 1359-1360.

PRUF—an acronym for Possibilistic Relational Universal Fuzzy—is a designation for a novel type of synthetic language which is intended to serve as a target language for the representation of meaning of expressions in a natural language. (Bibliographic Abstract only)

————, Fuzzy Set Theory—'A Perspective', in *Fuzzy Automata and Decision Processes*, Gupta, M.M., Saridis, G. N. and Gaines, B.R. (Eds.), New York: Elsevier North-Holland, (1977B), 3-4.

————, PRUF—A Meaning Representation Language for Natural Languages, *International Journal of Man-Machine Studies*, vol. 10, no. 4, (July 1978), 395-460. (Reprinted in [Mamdani and Gaines, 1981])

PRUF—an acronym for Possibilistic Relational Universal Fuzzy—is a meaning representation language for natural languages which departs from the conventional approaches to the theory of meaning in several important respects. First, a basic assumption underlying PRUF is that the imprecision that is intrinsic in natural languages is, for the most part, possibilistic rather than probabilistic in nature. Second, the logic underlying PRUF is not a two-valued or multi-valued logic, but a fuzzy logic in which the truth values are linguistic, that is, are of the form TRUE, NOT TRUE, MORE OR LESS TRUE, NOT VERY TRUE, etc., with each truth-value representing a fuzzy subset of the unit interval. Third, the quantifiers in PRUF—like the truth values—are allowed to be linguistic, i.e., may be expressed as MOST, MANY, FEW,

SOME, NOT VERY MANY, ALMOST ALL, etc. Based on the concept of the
cardinality of a fuzzy set, such quantifiers are given a concrete interpretation which
makes it possible to translate into PRUF propositons statements like "Many tall men
are much taller than most men," and "'All tall women are blonde' is not very true." The
concepts of semantic equivalence and semantic entailment in PRUF provide a basis for
question-answering and inference from fuzzy premises. In addition to serving as a
foundation for approximate reasoning, PRUF may be employed as a language for the
representation of imprecise knowledge and as a means of precise representation of
fuzzy propositions expressed in a natural language. (Bibliographic Abstract only)

———, Fuzzy Sets, in *Operations Research Support Methodology*, Holzman, A.G.
(Ed.), New York: Marcel Dekker, Inc., (1979A), 596-606.

A general description of fuzzy set theory for applications in operations research. A
sophisticated mathematical treatment.

———, Fuzzy Sets versus Probability, *Proceedings of the IEEE*, vol. 68, no. 3, (March
1980), 421.

In this paper Zadeh strongly disagrees with the opinions of other researchers who
argue that the theory of fuzzy sets is merely a disguised form of subjective probability.
He states:

In essence, the theory of fuzzy sets is aimed at the development of a body of
concepts and techniques for dealing with sources of uncertainty or imprecision which are nonstatistical in nature. For example, the proposition "X is a
small number" in which *small number* is a label of a fuzzy subset of nonnegative integers, defines the *possibility distribution* rather than the probability
distribution of X. What this implies is that if the degree to which an interger n
fits one's subjective perception of *small number* is m, then p, the possibility
that X may take n as its value, is numerically equal to m. Thus, the proposition "X is a small number," like the proposition "X is a number smaller than
5," conveys no information concerning the probability distribution of the
values of X. In this sense, the uncertainty associated with the proposition "X
is a small number" in nonstatistical in nature.

Zadeh then challenges the detractors of fuzzy set theory to solve a number of
problems using conventional logic and probability. One of those problems is: "If Mike
is much taller than most of his close friends, how tall is Mike?" He concludes by stating
that because of the unorthodox nature of fuzzy set theory, it

has been and continues to be controversial for some time. Eventually,
though, the theory of fuzzy sets is likely to be recognized as a natural
development in the evolution of scientific thinking. In retrospect, the skepti-
cism about its usefulness will be viewed as a manifestation of the human
attachment to tradition and resistance to innovation.

————, Possibility Theory and Soft Data Analysis. In *Mathematical Frontiers of the Social and Policy Sciences*, Cobb L. and Thrall, R.M. (Eds.), Boulder, Colorado: Westview Press, Inc. and American Association for the Advancement of Science, Washington, D.C., (1981A), 69–129.

An easy introduction to the foundations of PRUF [Zadeh, 1978], [Zadeh, 1981B]— possibility theory and possibility distributions.

————, Test-Score Semantics for Natural Languages and Meaning Representation Via PRUF, Computer Science Division, Department of Electrical Engineering and Computer Science and The Electronics Research Laboratory, University of California, Berkeley, California, Technical Report, (14 May 1981B).

This paper proposes a semantic method/theory for the meaning-representation language PRUF [Zadeh, 1978]. The basic strategy of this method is to define the meaning for, say, a proposition by (a) identifying the constraints which are induced by the proposition, (b) describing the tests that must be performed to ascertain the degree to which each constraint is satisfied, and (c) specifying the manner in which the degrees in question are to be aggregated to yield an overall test score.

Zimmermann, H.J. and Haley, K.B. Theory and Applications of Fuzzy Sets, *Operational Research '78*, Amsterdam: North-Holland, (1979).

A survey of the most interesting theoretical advances and applications of the recent past of the theory of fuzzy sets. Areas included are pattern recognition, automata theory, formal and natural languages, approximate reasoning, systems control, information theory, information processing, mathematical programming and medical applications.

AUTHOR INDEX

Adamo, J.M., 158
Addanki, S., 158
Aho, A.V., 131
Asa, K., 175
Atkinson, R., xii

Badre, A.N., 170
Baldwin, J.F., 158, 159, 172
Beeler, J., 159
Bellman, R., 8, 9, 10, 159, 160, 174, 181
Biller, W.F., 163, 180
Bonissone, P.P., 160
Bostic, K., 56
Braae, M., 160
Brownwell, H.H., 161, 166, 168
Bruce, A., 161
Burr, B., 84

Caramazza, A., 37, 40, 41, 81, 161, 166,
    167, 168, 177
Card, S.K., 84
Chang, S.K., 163, 179
Chaudhuri, E.B., 161
Clements, D.P., ix, 20, 24, 28, 30, 34, 45,
    48, 49, 54, 55, 79, 80, 161, 168, 180
Cobb, L., 185
Collins, A.M., 37
Colton, C.C., vi
Czogola, E., 162

Dagli, H.C., 81, 170
Dodds, D.R., 162
Donnell, M.L., 178, 180
Dubois, D.J., 40, 47, 162, 180

Efstathiou, J., 162, 176
Ellison, J.R., 163
Engel, S.E., 58
English, W.K., 84
Eshragh, F., 34, 163, 172
Evans, S.R., 95

Farrell, J., 95
Feagans, T.B., 163, 180

Fine, L.H., 164
Fischoff, B., 164
Fox, J., 164
Franksen, O.I., 164
Freeling, A.N.S., 164
Fu, K.S., 170, 183
Furuta, R., 95

Gaines, B.R., 155, 165, 166, 167, 170,
    172, 183
Gaskill, J.W., xii
Giertz, M., 8, 9, 10, 159, 174, 181
Giles, R., 165
Glucksberg, S., 37, 172
Goodman, G., 164
Goguen, J.A., 39, 166, 172
Goldberg, Adele, 83
Granda, R.E., 58
Guild, N.C.F., 159
Gupta, M.M., 20, 155, 165, 166, 167,
    168, 170, 173, 175, 180, 183

Haack, S., 167
Haley, K.B., 185
Hansen, W.J., 58
Harslem, E., 82, 84, 94, 95
Heider, E.R., 37, 167
Hersh, H.M., 37, 40, 41, 81, 166, 167,
    168, 177
Hoffman, L.J., ix, xii, 23, 35, 36, 82,
    168, 173
Horowitz, E., 135, 136

Information Policy, Inc., 43, 168
Irby, C., 82, 84, 94, 95
Ireland, T., xii

Jain, R., 168, 169, 180
Johannsen, G., 169

Kandel, A.M., 169
Kaufmann, A., 5, 16, 82, 167, 169, 170
Kelvin, Lord, 19
Kickert, J.M., 170

SUBJECT INDEX